AN INTRODUCTION TO
FUNCTIONAL PROGRAMMING WITH SCHEME

NANCY LYNN TINKHAM

Rowan University

Linus
Publications, Inc.

Published by Linus Publications, Inc.

Deer Park, NY 11729

ISBN 1-934188-99-9

Printed in the United States of America.

10 9 8 7 6 5 4 3 2 1

TABLE OF CONTENTS

Chapter 0: What is this book about?

What this book is about

This book is an introduction to the functional programming paradigm and the Scheme programming language. It is designed for students in an undergraduate Programming Languages course. Because a semester course in Programming Languages typically cannot spend more than two or three weeks on any given language, this book has deliberately been kept short, so that students can realistically read all of the material in a few days.

The reader is assumed to have some prior experience programming in another high-level language, and to have some familiarity with recursion and linked lists.

For the reader who wishes to go on to master Scheme in its entirety, several textbooks and Scheme language reference books are listed in chapter 8.

How to use this book

When reading textbooks, it is tempting to read the text and skip over the exercises. Do not do this. Think of the exercises as an integral part of the text. *Do every exercise in every section.* Most of the exercises are short, so this task is not as time-consuming as it might appear. The exercises are there to make sure you've absorbed what's in one section before going on to the next, and to clarify subtle points. Solutions to all the exercises are given in Appendix 1, so you can check your work.

In addition to the exercises, some longer programming projects without solutions are provided. These let you combine the tools you've learned and apply them creatively to larger problems.

Acknowledgements

I am grateful to Lincoln Bennett, Carol Bolton, Ariel Calderon, Kiacha Christy, Loc Do, Douglas Eaton, Robert Elliott, Keith Hansen, Marcus Langston, Craig Muller, Darren Provine, Zimmy Shah, Bernard Sypniewski, and Richard Wallace for their comments on earlier drafts of the manuscript, and to my Programming Languages students at Rowan for their feedback and their patience. I am also indebted to Bruce Ballard and John Hayward, who first introduced me to LISP.

In the Programming Projects section, Seth Bergmann suggested the problem about reflexive transitive closure, and Darren Provine suggested the problems about dates.

This document was written using *vi* and typeset with *groff.* The index was prepared using *makeindex*. Figures were created with *xfig* and the *GNU Image Manipulation Program (GIMP)*.

Chapter 1: Functional Programming

Most of the widely-used programming languages — C, C++, Ada, COBOL, FORTRAN, and so on — are very similar in style. Programs in these languages are sequences of commands; the data in the programs are stored in variables, which are given initial values and which are then updated with new values as the computation proceeds. This programming language paradigm is called the **imperative programming paradigm** or the **procedural programming paradigm**.

This is not the only approach to programming, however. One alternative is the **functional programming paradigm**. Functional programming is built around the idea of functions and function composition: the elementary building blocks of a functional programming language are small, simple functions, and large programs are constructed by writing functions which call other functions, which call other functions, and so on. This is similar to defining a complicated function in mathematics by putting smaller functions together: $f(x, y) = (x - 1)^2 + (y + 1)^2$ is computed by composing the subtraction, addition, and exponentiation functions, for example.

Historically, before modern digital computers existed, mathematicians proposed several different models of computation, in an attempt to formalize the process of computing so that it could be carried out on a computing machine. Several of these models (the Turing Machine, for instance) used the idea of a sequence of commands which stored data in a collection of machine memory locations; these models gave rise to the imperative programming languages. Several of the models used other approaches, however, such as collections of grammar rules (Post systems and Markov algorithms, for example) or functions (Partial Recursive Functions and Church's Lambda Calculus, for example). Eventually (and remarkably!), all of these models were eventually proved to be equivalent to each other in computing power.

The Lambda Calculus, which begins with a collection of elementary functions and uses rules for function composition for building more complicated calculations, inspired both the programming paradigm and some of the notation that are used by the programming languages LISP and Scheme.

1.1. A historical look at LISP and Scheme

The programming language LISP was designed by John McCarthy in the late 1950s and early 1960s as a tool for his artificial intelligence (AI) research. At the time, the major high-level programming languages were FORTRAN, COBOL, and ALGOL, all of which are ill-suited to many of the programming problems that arise in AI. AI is the branch of computer science that attempts to make computers solve puzzles, play games, converse in English, learn, prove theorems, and perform similar tasks that are considered to be "intelligent" when humans do them. Many of these problems involve manipulation of lists of symbols, which was difficult to implement in the languages that existed in the 1950s and early 1960s. Thus, McCarthy designed his own programming language called LISP (which stand for LISt Processing), in which symbols and lists were built-in elements of the language. LISP quickly became popular in the AI community, and it is still widely used today for AI work.

In the 1960s and 1970s, dialects of LISP proliferated as many different universities and other research sites customized LISP for their own preferences and machines. Most of these dialects had the word "LISP" in the name — "VAX LISP", "Franz LISP", and so on. Eventually, attempts were made to consolidate the dialects into just one or two LISP versions, so that the language would be more standardized. Currently, there are two widely-used LISP dialects: Common LISP (Guy L. Steele, Jr., 1984), and Scheme (Gerald Jay Sussman and Guy L. Steele, Jr., 1975). Thus, Scheme — despite its unusual name — is a version of LISP, and most of what is said in this paper about Scheme will be true of Common LISP and other LISP dialects as well.

The official specification for the most recent version of Scheme is the *Revised^5 Report on the Algorithmic Language Scheme*, available at http://www.sonic.net/~bear/scheme/r5rs.html . The superscript 5 means that this is the fifth revision of Scheme since its original creation; the previous version was the *Revised^4 Report*, and the next one (if the language is revised further) will be the *Revised^6 Report*.

The IEEE also maintains a standard for Scheme: IEEE Standard 1178-1990, *IEEE Standard for the Scheme Programming Language*. A copy can be ordered from http://standards.ieee.org/

1.2. The Scheme notation for functions

In mathematics, several different notations are used for functions. Many functions are written using **prefix notation**, in which the function symbol comes before the arguments:

    sin(x)
    log(x)
    f(x,y)

Some binary functions are written using **infix notation**, in which the function symbol comes in between the two arguments:

    x + y
    x - y

A few functions are written using **postfix notation**, in which the function symbol comes after two arguments:

    x^2

And some functions are written using other notations:

    $\sqrt{x}$
    $|x|$

Scheme uses **prefix notation** consistently, for all its functions. This looks a little strange when applied to functions like **+**, but the notation is consistent and thus easy to remember, once you get used to it.

Additionally, Scheme places parentheses differently from most mathematical notation: an expression with a function call begins with a left parenthesis, followed by the function symbol, followed by the arguments (separated by white space — no commas), ending with a right parenthesis. For example, $\sqrt{9}$ is written (sqrt 9) in Scheme, $4 + 6$ is written (+ 4 6), and $\dfrac{10 - 3}{2}$ is written (/ (- 10 3) 2).

Exercises: Scheme notation

Answers to all of the exercises are given in Appendix 1.

1. Convert each of the following Scheme expressions into conventional mathematical notation.

    a. `(+ (sqrt x) 5)`

    b. `(* (- x y) (+ z 2))`

    c. `(/ 10 (- (+ x 1) y))`

    d. `(sqrt (* 2 x))`

    e. `(abs (/ (+ y 2) (- x 1)))`

2. Convert each of the following mathematical expressions into Scheme notation.

    a. $5(x + y)$

    b. $xy - xz$

    c. $\dfrac{2x}{3}$

    d. $\dfrac{10(x + 5)}{y - 1}$

    e. $\sqrt{16x - 3y}$

Chapter 2: Language Basics

In this chapter we look at the most elementary components of Scheme: lexical issues (identifier format and basic layout of expressions) and data types.

2.1. Lexical conventions

An identifier in Scheme can contain letters, digits, or any of the following characters:

$$! \ \$ \ \% \ \& \ * \ + \ - \ . \ / \ : \ < \ = \ > \ ? \ @ \ \hat{} \ \_ \ \~{}$$

Identifiers cannot begin with any of the characters that begin numbers (digits, ., +, or -), but identifiers can begin with any other character. An exception to this rule is that +, -, and ... are identifiers. There is no limit on the length of an identifier. Thus,

```
x
total_income
x$%2
*sum*
This_is_a_very_very_long_identifier
```

are all legal Scheme identifiers.

Some Scheme interpreters will accept other combinations of characters as identifiers, allowing identifiers to contain or start with more characters than those listed above, but all Scheme interpreters are required to accept at least the identifiers described in the preceding paragraph.

White space is insignificant in Scheme, as it is in most modern programming languages, except in a few obvious situations: identifiers must be separated by either white space or parentheses or both (so that the computer can tell the difference between a variable called xy and two adjacent variables x y); and a space cannot occur in the middle of an identifier (x y is not a legal variable or parameter name). Thus,

```
(- (*
         4         5)
  2)
```

is a legal Scheme expression, evaluating to 18.

If a semicolon (;) occurs in a line of Scheme code, then the remainder of that line will be interpreted as a **comment**. For example,

```
(— (*
              4            5)    ; This is a comment.
      2)                         ; So is this.
```

is also a legal Scheme expression, evaluating to 18.

Scheme is not case-sensitive: a and A are considered to be the same symbol. (This is the official position of the *Revised⁵ Report on the Algorithmic Language Scheme*; a few implementations, however, depart from this standard by being case-sensitive.)

2.2. Data types

Scheme uses dynamic type binding for its variables and parameters; that is, unlike many conventional languages such as C or C++, Scheme programs do not contain declarations for the data types of variables and parameters; instead, the type of a variable or parameter is determined at run-time. A function can be called at one time with a number as an argument, and at a later time with a list or string as an argument, without any error resulting; the parameter's type is determined by the type of the argument during each different function call.

The most important types of Scheme data objects are atoms and lists.

2.2.1. Atoms

Atoms in Scheme can be symbols, strings, or numbers.

Symbols are represented by identifiers. apple, a, x12$, and ** are examples of legal Scheme symbols.

True is represented in Scheme by the symbol #T, and *false* by the symbol #F. Strictly speaking, any value other than #F is considered *true*; apple, 32, and (a b c) are, therefore, all considered *true*.‡

Strings are sequences of characters surrounded by double quotes. A string may contain any character. "Fred" and "ab.c" are examples of legal Scheme strings. Note that the string "apple" is different from the symbol apple, and the string "123" is different from the number 123.

Numbers may be integers, rational numbers, real numbers, or complex numbers. Each of these types is considered a subtype of the types that follow it in the list; thus, every integer is also rational, real, and complex; every rational is also real and complex; and every real is complex. 50, -77, 3.14, .8, 1/3, and 10+3i are examples of legal Scheme numbers: 50 and -77 are integers; 3.14 and .8 are real; 1/3 is rational; and 10+3i is complex. Many Scheme implementations support arbitrary precision integers: integers may contain any number of digits, and all the digits will be significant.

---

‡ Most other dialects of LISP use the symbols t for *true* and nil (i.e., the empty list) for *false*. The *Revised⁵ Report* allows Scheme to differ from other LISP versions on this point, so that nil, the empty list, and #F are allowed to be three distinct symbols in Scheme. Some Scheme implementations, however, allow t and nil as symbols for *true* and *false*, for compatibility with other LISP dialects.

2.2.2. Lists

Lists are a built-in data type in Scheme. The programmer does not need to allocate space and manipulate pointers explicitly when working with lists; this is done automatically.

To specify a list in Scheme, write the elements inside parentheses, separated by white space (no commas):

```
(a b c)
(apple banana persimmon kiwi strawberry)
("Adam"  "Barbara"  "Carl"  "Donna")
```

Lists can contain nested lists:

```
(a (b c) ((d (e))) f)
```

Lists can contain a mixture of data types:

```
(apple 3 "Fred" 2.7)
```

The empty list† is written as an empty pair of parentheses: ( ).

Exercises

1. Which of the following are legal Scheme identifiers?

    a. 3+4

    b. a+b

    c. total$

    d. -total

    e. $total

2. Classify each of the following constants as a *symbol*, a *string*, a *number*, or *not a legal constant*.

    a. "3/5"

    b. 3/5

    c. three/5

    d. 3/"five"

    e. three_fifths

    f. 35

---

† In most LISP dialects, the empty list can also be written as the special symbol `nil`, but Scheme does not support this.

Chapter 3: Calling Built-In Functions

Scheme contains a large number of predefined functions for mathematical calculation and list manipulation.

3.1. Arithmetic

The arithmetic functions are represented by conventional symbols: +, -, *, and /. Some other mathematical functions are standard as well: for example, square root is written `sqrt`, absolute value is written `abs`, and remainder after division is written `remainder`.

Examples:

Expression:	Return value:
`(+ 3 8)`	11
`(- 12 5)`	7
`(* 7 3)`	21
`(/ 8 2)`	4
`(sqrt 25)`	5
`(abs -7)`	7

3.2. Quote

Quote is a function that returns its argument unevaluated. For example,

```
(quote (+ 4 6))
```

returns the list

```
(+ 4 6)
```

instead of performing the addition. Similarly,

```
(quote +)
```

returns the symbol

```
+
```

without attempting to interpret **+** as a function. `Quote` is useful whenever you want to talk about a literal symbol or expression, instead of the result of evaluating that symbol or expression.

As it turns out, `quote` is a very commonly-used function — so commonly used, in fact, that an abbreviation is provided for it. Instead of writing `quote`, a single quote is used, and the outer parentheses are dropped:

`(quote (+ 4 6))`	may be written as `'(+ 4 6)`
`(quote +)`	may be written as `'+`

Nancy Lynn Tinkham

3.3. Taking lists apart: Car and Cdr

Since the list is the most important built-in data structure in Scheme, Scheme provides functions for manipulating lists. A pair of functions for breaking lists apart into their components is **car** and **cdr**.

The function car takes one list as an argument and returns the first element of that list.

Examples:

Expression:	Return value:
(car '(a b c d))	a
(car '(red blue green))	red
(car '(+ 3 5))	+
(car '(purple))	purple
(car '((a b) c (d (e))))	(a b)

The function cdr (pronounced "could-er") takes one list as an argument and returns the result of removing the first argument from that list.

Examples:

Expression:	Return value:
(cdr '(a b c d))	(b c d)
(cdr '(red blue green))	(blue green)
(cdr '(+ 3 5))	(3 5)
(cdr '(purple))	( )
(cdr '((a b) c (d (e))))	(c (d (e)))

Car and cdr can be combined to extract components from the middle of a list:

Expression:	Return value:
(car (cdr '(a b c d)))	b
(cdr (cdr '(red blue green)))	(green)
(cdr (car (cdr (cdr '((a b) c (d e f) g)))))	(e f)
(car (car '((a b) c (d (e))))	a

Because combinations of car and cdr are frequently used in this way, an abbreviation is provided: begin with **c**, end with **r**, and fill in the middle with **a** for each car and **d** for each cdr, left to right. For example, (cadr x) means (car (cdr x)), and (cddadr x) means (cdr (cdr (car (cdr x)))). These can contain up to four **a**s and **d**s.

Examples:

Expression:	Return value:
`(cadr '(a b c d))`	`b`
`(cddr '(red blue green))`	`(green)`
`(cdaddr '((a b) c (d e f) g))`	`(e f)`
`(caar '((a b) c (d (e))))`	`a`

3.4. Constructing lists: Cons

The basic function for putting elements together to form a list is **cons**. The function call

`(cons x y)`

returns the list whose `car` is *x* and whose `cdr` is *y*. Viewed another way, `(cons x y)` returns the result of inserting element *x* at the beginning of list *y*.

Examples:

Expression:	Return value:
`(cons 'a '(b c d))`	`(a b c d)`
`(cons 'elephant '(giraffe lion))`	`(elephant giraffe lion)`
`(cons 'apple '( ))`	`(apple)`
`(cons '(a b) '(c d))`	`((a b) c d)`

Note especially the last example. The first argument to `cons` may be a list (in this case, `(a b)`), in which case the list becomes the first element of the returned list. Observe that `cons` is not append: `(cons '(a b) '(c d))` does *not* return `(a b c d)`.

Exercises: car, cdr, and cons

Evaluate each of the following expressions.

1. `(car '(lion (tiger cheetah) leopard))`
2. `(cdr '(lion (tiger cheetah) leopard))`
3. `(car '((bear fox) (wolf)))`
4. `(cdr '((bear fox) (wolf)))`
5. `(cdr '(elephant giraffe))`
6. `(car (cdr '(lemur gorilla orangutan)))`
7. `(cdr (cdr (cdr '(leopard cougar tiger lion bobcat))))`
8. `(caadr '(deer (antelope) giraffe moose))`
9. `(cdaar '(((horse zebra) (lion cheetah)) (wolf coyote)))`
10. `(cons 'fox '(bear rabbit))`
11. `(cons '(lion tiger) '(giraffe antelope))`

12. `(car (cons 'lion '(tiger)))`

13. `(cdr (cons 'lion '(tiger)))`

14. `(cons 'squirrel (cons 'fox (cons 'rabbit '( ))))`

15. `(cons (car '(lion tiger leopard)) (cdr '(elephant giraffe zebra)))`

16. Write an expression containing the list `(a b (c (d) e))` and any combination of `car` and `cdr`, which returns the value b.

17. Write an expression containing the list `(a b (c (d) e))` and any combination of `car` and `cdr`, which returns the value e.

18. Write an expression containing the list `(a b (c (d) e))` and any combination of `car` and `cdr`, which returns the value d.

3.5. Predicates

A predicate is a function that returns true or false. Scheme has a number of built-in predicates, including the following:

Predicate	Meaning	Example returning #T	Example returning #F
null?	Returns #T if its argument is the empty list; #F otherwise	(null? '( ))	(null? '(a b c))
eq?	Returns #T if arguments are identical symbols; #F otherwise. (But see below for details.)	(eq? 'a 'a)	(eq? 'a 'b) (eq? 4 4.0)
eqv?	Returns #T if arguments are atoms with the same value; #F otherwise	(eqv? 'a 'a) (eqv? "apple" "apple")	(eqv? 'a 'b) (eqv? 4 4.0)
equal?	Returns #T if arguments have the same value; #F otherwise	(equal? 'a 'a) (equal? "apple" "apple") (equal? '(a) '(a))	(equal? 'a 'b) (equal? 4 4.0)
=	Mathematical equality	(= 1 1) (= 4 4.0)	(= 1 2)
symbol?	Returns #T if argument is a symbol; #F otherwise	(symbol? 'apple)	(symbol? "apple")
string?	Returns #T if argument is a string; #F otherwise	(string? "apple")	(string? 'apple)
number?	Returns #T if argument is a number; #F otherwise	(number? 33)	(number? 'apple)
complex?	Returns #T if argument is a complex number; #F otherwise	(complex? 2+5i)	(complex? 'apple)
real?	Returns #T if argument is a real number; #F otherwise	(real? 33.5)	(real? 2+5i)
rational?	Returns #T if argument is a rational number; #F otherwise	(rational? 3/7)	(rational? 2+5i)
integer?	Returns #T if argument is an integer; #F otherwise	(integer? 33)	(integer? 1.5)
list?	Returns #T if argument is a list; #F otherwise.	(list? '(a b c))	(list? 'apple)
pair?	Returns #T if argument is a pair; #F otherwise. (A list is a special kind of pair; see chapter 4)	(pair? '(a b c))	(pair? 'apple)

Predicate names usually end in a ?. The predicate null? is provided because checking for the empty list occurs frequently in Scheme programs; the empty list often serves as the base case for a recursive function definition, for example.

There are four different equality predicates. `eq?` returns #T if its two arguments are exactly identical; it is often implemented by checking whether the two items are stored at the same location in memory. `eq?` is most appropriate for checking two symbols for equality: given two identical symbols, `eq?` will return #T, and given two different symbols, `eq?` will return #F. The behavior of `eq?` on numbers, strings, and lists is implementation-dependent.

`eqv?` returns #T if its two arguments are atoms with the same value; `eqv?` will return #T for symbols, strings, and identical numbers. Note, however, that (eqv? 4 4.0) will return #F, as the integer 4 and the real 4.0 are different objects. The behavior of `eqv?` on lists is implementation-dependent.

`equal?` returns #T if its two arguments have the same value. It is the most "generous" of the equality checks: lists with the same value will return #T, as well as symbols, numbers, and strings. As with `eqv?`, however, (equal? 4 4.0) returns #F.

The predicate `=` checks for mathematical equality, and it performs the appropriate type conversions if its arguments are of different numerical types. (= 4 4.0) returns #T.

Because Scheme has a very weak sense of type, one cannot simply look at a variable or parameter declaration to determine an object's data type. For situations where the data type needs to be known (e.g., before performing a mathematical evaluation), Scheme provides a collection of predicates that return #T if the argument is of the specified type, and return #F otherwise: `symbol?`, `string?`, `number?`, `list?`, and `pair?`.

The relational predicates in Scheme are `=` (equal), `<` (less than), `>` (greater than), `<=` (less than or equal), and `>=` (greater than or equal).

Scheme includes the functions `and`, `or`, and `not` for building complex logical conditions. And and `or` can take any number of arguments; `and` returns true if all of its arguments are true, and `or` returns true if at least one of its arguments is true.† Not takes one argument; it returns true if its argument is false, and false if its argument is true. Thus,

```
(and (> 4 5) (< 2 10))                    returns #F
(and (= 2 2) (<= 8 10) (> 9 7))           returns #T
(or (> 4 5) (< 2 10))                     returns #T
(or (= 2 2) (<= 8 10) (> 9 7))            returns #T
(not (< 2 10))                            returns #F
```

3.6. Other built-in functions

Scheme has many built-in functions, which are described in the references in chapter 8 (*For Further Reading*). Three of the more useful ones for working with lists are:

(member Item L)

Returns the portion of list *L* that begins with the first occurrence of *Item* in *L*; returns #F if *Item* is not a member of *L*. E.g., (member 'b '(a b c)) returns (b c), and (member 'd '(a b c)) returns #F. Note that these return values can be interpreted

---

† In a little more detail, and returns the value of the last argument, if all its arguments are true, and returns #F otherwise; or returns the value of its first true argument, if one of its arguments is true, and returns #F otherwise. Because all non-#F values are considered true, this has the effect of making and and or return true or false values in the expected way, but allows the *true* return value to contain more information than simply #T.

as true/false values.

(list Element1 Element2 ...)

Takes any number of elements. Returns a list containing *Element1*, *Element2*, ..., in the order specified. E.g., (list 'a 'b 'c) returns (a b c).

(append List1 List2 List3 ...)

Returns the result of appending the specified lists. For example, (append '(a b) '(c) '(d e)) returns (a b c d e).

3.7. A sample Scheme interpreter session

Below is a sample session with a typical Scheme interpreter. The interpreter's prompt in this example is > ; the exact prompt used will differ from one interpreter to the next.

The Scheme interpreter repeatedly reads an expression from the keyboard, evaluates the expression, and prints the result on the screen.

```
> (+ 4 5)
9
> (quote (+ 4 5))
(+ 4 5)
> '(+ 4 5)
(+ 4 5)
> (car '(a b c))
a
> (cdr '(a b c))
(b c)
> (define (f x) (* x x))
> (f 5)
25
```

In the first line, the computer evaluates the expression (+ 4 5), returning the value 9. The next expression, (quote (+ 4 5)), asks for (+ 4 5) to be returned unevaluated. Replacing quote by a single quote mark also returns (+ 4 5) unevaluated.

The next two expressions illustrate the use of list operators car and cdr. The appropriate portion of the list is constructed and returned.

The expression (define (f x) (* x x)) defines a new function f, with one parameter, which returns the square of its argument. (The exact syntax for defining Scheme functions will be explained in chapter 5.) A define expression in Scheme has an unimportant return value and, additionally, an important side effect: the function named in the define expression is created, so that, in this example, the function f can now be called as though it were a built-in function. This is illustrated in the next expression: (f 5) computes and returns the value 25, in accordance with the previous define expression.

Chapter 4: List Implementation

Lists are implemented in Scheme using two-part cells — called *cons* cells, because one of these cells is created each time `cons` is called. The first component of the cell points to the *car* of the list; the second component of the cell points to the *cdr* of the list. The empty list is represented by a nil pointer. Thus, for example, the list (a) is implemented:

Either component may point to additional *cons* cells. For example, the list (a b c) is implemented:

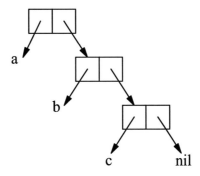

Note that lists have a "backbone" of cells beginning at the first cell in the list, proceeding down to the right along *cdr* links, and ending in *nil*; the first cell in the backbone points to the first element in the list, the second cell to the second element, and so on.

For a more complicated example, consider (a (b c) d):

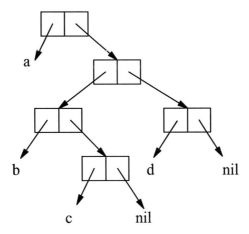

Since this is a three-element list, the "backbone" contains three cells: the first points to a, the second to the list (b c), and the third to d.

Similarly, the list ((a) (b c) d) is implemented as:

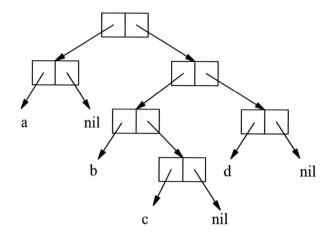

with the *car* of the first cell now pointing to the list (a).

Occasionally, new Scheme programmers will type

```
(cons 'a 'b)
```

intending to create the list (a b). Instead of (a b), the interpreter will print (a . b). This strange-looking expression represents the structure

That is, (a . b) is not a list at all, but rather a structure whose *car* is a and whose *cdr* is b. A structure like this is called a "dotted pair". While dotted pairs are sometimes used deliberately by programmers (for example, if one has data represented as a list of pairs, one can use dotted pairs instead of two-element lists to implement the pairs more compactly), beginning Scheme programmers more often produce dotted pairs accidentally, by forgetting that, to produce a list, the second argument to cons must be either ( ) or a nonempty list. If you find your Scheme program producing dotted pairs where you didn't expect them, check the cons statements in the program for places where an atom is used as the second argument to a cons expression.

The built-in predicate pair? returns #T if its argument is a pair: that is, a structure containing *cons* cells. A list is a special type of pair in which all the *cons* cell "backbones" end in *nil* when the rightward links are followed to the end.

Incidentally, the *cons* cell implementation of lists helps to explain the odd names *car* and *cdr* for the two portions of a list. The first LISP system was implemented on an IBM 704, whose memory cells could be divided into an "address register" and a "decrement register". Each *cons* cell was implemented using one of these two-part memory cells. Hence, the *car* of a list is the **C**ontents *of the* **A**ddress **R**egister, and the *cdr* of a list is the **C**ontents *of the* **D**ecrement **R**egister. Even though the IBM 704 is now obsolete, LISP programmers got used to calling these functions *car* and *cdr*, and the names have persisted.

Exercises: List Implementation

1. `(cons 'a 'b)` is not the correct way to create the list `(a b)`. Give an expression using `cons`, a, b, and any other components you find necessary, which will return the list `(a b)`.

2. Draw the structure that implements the list `(a ((b) c) (d e))`.

3. Draw the structure that implements the list `((a b) (c d))`.

4. What list corresponds to this structure?

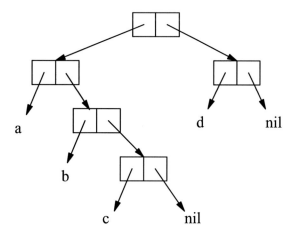

5. What list corresponds to this structure?

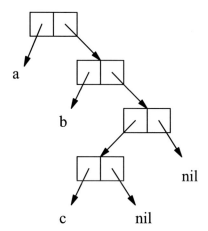

Chapter 5: Defining Your Own Functions

There are three forms for defining your own functions in Scheme. Of these, the third is used most of the time, but all three will be described here. All three forms use `define`.

5.1. Defining a new function by renaming an existing function

To give a new name to an existing function, use this format:

```
(define new_name old_name)
```

For example, if you would rather use the function names `first` and `rest` in place of `car` and `cdr`, you can define the new names this way:

```
(define first car)
(define rest cdr)
```

With these definitions in place, you can now use the new names as though they were built-in functions:

```
> (first '(a b c))
a
> (rest '(a b c))
(b c)
```

5.2. Defining a new function: long form

There are two forms for defining a new function. The first and longer form uses a format based directly on the Lambda Calculus notation. A function written for the Lambda Calculus uses this format:

$$\lambda xy(x * x + y * y)$$

The symbol λ announces the parameter list; the list of parameters is then followed by the rule for calculating the function (in this case, the function returns $x^2 + y^2$).

Scheme notation is similar:

```
(define f (lambda (x y) (+ (* x x) (* y y))))
```

The word `define` is followed by the name of the new function, which is followed by an expression defining the function; the expression is the word `lambda`, followed by the parameter list, followed by the rule for the function:

```
(define function_name (lambda (parameters)
     expression  expression ... ))
```

Each *expression* is evaluated in order, and the value of the last *expression* is the value that will be returned by the function.

5.3. Defining a new function: short form

Because the *lambda* notation is a bit longwinded, a shorter form can be used for defining functions. The previous function f, defined using the shorter notation, becomes:

```
(define (f x y) (+ (* x x) (* y y)))
```

In general, the form is:

```
(define (function_name argument argument ... )
    expression
    expression
    ...
    expression
)
```

This defines a function with name *function_name* and a sequence of arguments; each of the expressions is evaluated, in order, and then the value of the last expression is returned as the return value of the function.

Ordinarily, only one expression appears in the body of the function:

```
(define (function_name argument argument ... )
    expression
)
```

and the value of *expression* is the return value of the function. The longer form is provided in case one wishes to include expressions with useful side effects. For example, if one wanted to have a function display some output in addition to returning a value, one could call an output function such as display (which prints its argument on the screen) or newline (which prints a new line) to display output before computing the return value.

```
(define (f x)
    (display "The value of x is ")
    (display x)
    (newline)
    (* x x)
)
```

This version of f prints some information about the argument x before returning x^2. When f is called, it will print the following:

```
> (f 4)
The value of x is 4
16
>
```

The first line (The value of x is 4) is printed by the calls to display and newline in the function; the second line (16) is the return value of the function, as printed in the ordinary way by the Scheme interpreter.

Some of the basic **input/output** functions are the following:

(read)
> Returns a Scheme expression read from the keyboard.

(write x)
> Writes expression x to the screen.

(display x)
> Writes expression x to the screen in a human-readable format, omitting double quotes around strings.

(newline)
> Writes a newline to the screen.

Exercises: Writing simple functions

1. Write a Scheme function `tri_area` which takes two arguments, the base and height of a triangle, and returns the area of the triangle. (Area may be computed with the formula $a = \frac{1}{2} bh$.)

    For example, `(tri_area 10 3)` should return 15.

2. Write a Scheme function `avg4` which takes four arguments and returns the average of the four arguments.

    For example, `(avg4 6 3 7 2)` should return the rational number 9/2.

5.4. Control constructs

Aside from ordinary function calls, two of the most important control constructs in Scheme are the `cond` statement, which provides a multi-way branch, and recursion, which provides repetition.

5.4.1. Cond

The most important branching construct in Scheme is `cond`. A `cond` expression returns one of several different possible values, based on a sequence of true/false conditions.

The general form for `cond` is:

```
(cond    (predicate   expression   expression   ...)
         (predicate   expression   expression   ...)
         ...
         (predicate   expression   expression   ...)
)
```

That is, the word `cond` is followed by a sequence of lists. Each list begins with a predicate (that is, a function that returns true or false) and continues with one or more expressions.

The meaning of a `cond` expression is:

> Evaluate each of the predicates in order, from the first to the last, until a predicate is found that returns **true**. When this predicate is found, evaluate each of the expressions in that predicate's list, and then return the value of the last

expression as the value of the overall `cond` expression. If no predicate evaluates to true, the value of the `cond` expression is undefined.

`Cond` expression are usually simpler than one might guess from looking at the general form listed above. Most of the time, each predicate is followed by only one expression, so that the form is:

```
(cond    (predicate  expression)
         (predicate  expression)
         . . .
         (predicate  expression)
)
```

This simpler form means:

> Evaluate each of the predicates in order, from the first to the last, until a predicate is found that returns **true**. When this predicate is found, return the value of the corresponding expression as the value of the overall `cond` expression. If no predicate evaluates to true, the value of the `cond` expression is undefined.

As with `define`, `cond` allows multiple expressions so that expressions with useful side effects (such as `display`) can be included.

As a first example of a `cond` statement, consider a function (`maximum x y`) that returns the maximum of its two arguments. There are two cases: if $x \geq y$, then the function should return x; if $x < y$, then the function should return y. This gives us:

```
(define (maximum x y)
    (cond    ((>= x y) x)
             (#T y)))
```

(As it happens, Scheme already has a function `max` which returns the maximum of its arguments. Thus, if you wish to type in and test this code, make sure to give it a name different from `max`, such as `maximum`.)

As a second example, consider a function (`classify x`) which returns one of the symbols `negative`, `zero`, or `positive`, depending on which category its argument x falls into. Note that in this case we have a 3-way branch, not merely a 2-way branch. `Cond` easily handles three or more conditions:

```
(define (classify x)
    (cond    ((< x 0) 'negative)
             ((= x 0) 'zero)
             (#T 'positive)))
```

Since a `cond` expression is undefined if no predicate evaluates to true, it is important to ensure that at least one predicate will be true. A common way to do this is to use #T as the last predicate in the list, so that this last predicate is guaranteed to be *true* even if none of the others is. Note that this was done in the `maximum` and `classify` examples above.

Scheme provides an alternative notation for #T in the context of a `cond` expression: The word `else`, when used as a predicate in a `cond` expression, means the same thing as #T; that is, it evaluates to *true*. Using this notation, the previous examples become:

```scheme
(define (maximum x y)
    (cond    ((>= x y) x)
             (else y)))

(define (classify x)
    (cond    ((< x 0) 'negative)
             ((= x 0) 'zero)
             (else 'positive)))
```

Exercises: Writing functions using cond

1.   Write a Scheme function (how_big N) which returns one of the following strings:

"small"	if N is 10 or smaller
"medium"	if N is bigger than 10 but no bigger than 20
"big"	if N is bigger than 20 but less than 100
"very big"	if N is 100 or bigger
"not a number"	if N is not a number

2.   Write a Scheme function tax with two parameters, marital status (*m* or *s*) and income, which will return the amount of tax due, computed according to the tax table below:

	Single	Married
Income ≤ 50000	15% of income	10% of income
Income > 50000	25% of income	20% of income

5.4.2. Recursion

While Scheme does have a limited looping construct, repetition in programs is generally achieved through recursion.

Recursion in Scheme, as in other programming languages, involves one or more *base cases* — simple cases in which a value can be returned without any recursion — and one or more *recursive cases* — cases in which the function calls itself in order to compute the return value. Since the choice of a base case or recursive case is a conditional selection, recursion will usually occur in combination with a cond expression.

In general, the trick to constructing a recursive function is to break down the problem into pieces, some of which are smaller instances of the same kind of problem as the original. For instance, in the first example below (sumlist), we want to find the sum of the numbers in a list L. To solve this, we will break the list into its car and its cdr. Finding the sum of the cdr of L is the same kind of problem as the original: we want to find the sum of the numbers in a list. Thus, we can solve this subproblem by calling sumlist recursively on the cdr of L.

5.4.2.1. Numeric List Functions

One commonly-occurring pattern in recursive Scheme functions is traversing a list and performing some kind of arithmetic function on each item in the list (adding up numbers, multiplying numbers, counting selected items in the list, etc.), returning the overall number that results.

For these functions, the base case is often the empty list. In the recursive case, the most common pattern is to split the list into its `car` and its `cdr`, call the function recursively on the `cdr`, and then combine the `car` of the list with the number returned by the function in some fashion to determine the overall result.

Example: Computing the sum of a list

As an illustration, consider a function `sumlist` to compute the sum of a list. For example, `(sumlist '(2 4 6))` should return 12, and `(sumlist '(10 8 1 3 1))` should return 23.

In Scheme, this function can be written:

```
(define (sumlist L)
    (cond    ((null? L) 0)
             (else (+ (car L) (sumlist (cdr L)))))))
```

This should be read as saying:

> If list L is empty,
>> then the sum of the numbers in L is 0.
> Otherwise, to find the sum of the numbers in L,
>> add the first number in L to the sum of the rest of the numbers in L.

Example: Counting the number of occurrences of an item in a list

A second illustration is function `occurs`, which counts the number of occurrences of a given item in a list. Some sample calls to function `occurs` are `(occurs 'a '(a b a c a a))`, which returns 4 (since a occurs in (a b a c a a) 4 times), and `(occurs 'b '(c d e))`, which returns 0.

As before, the base case will be the empty list. The function will return 0 in this case, since any possible item occurs 0 times in the empty list. There will be two recursive cases, since there are two possibilities for a nonempty list: the item matches the `car` of the list, or it does not. In both cases, we will want to call `occurs` recursively to determine the number of times the item occurs in the `cdr` of the list. Having done that, we will add 1 to the count if the item matched the `car`, and add nothing if the item did not match the `car`.

This gives us the following Scheme implementation:

```
(define (occurs item L)
    (cond    ((null? L) 0)
             ((equal? item (car L)) (+ 1 (occurs item (cdr L))))
             (else (occurs item (cdr L))))))
```

5.4.2.2. Predicates

A predicate is a function that returns true or false. A predicate that takes one or more lists of unknown length as arguments will ordinarily use recursion to process the list. The base case(s) will return #T or #F; the recursive cases use the truth value returned by the recursive call, often together with another boolean function call and a boolean connective (and, or, or not) to determine the truth value to be returned by the function.

Example: Determining whether all list elements are even

As an example of writing a predicate, consider a function (all_even L) which returns #T if every number in list L is even, and #F otherwise. (For simplicity, we will assume that L is a list containing only numbers, with no nested lists. For example, (all_even '(4 10 2)) should return #T, and (all_even '(8 3 5 4)) should return #F.

The empty list will be a base case: (all_even '( )) returns #T. Of the nonempty cases, one allows the function to return a value immediately, and the other requires recursion: if the first number in the list is odd, then all_even should return #F; but if the first number is even, then the remainder of the list must be inspected to determine the return value.

The function, therefore, looks like this:

```
(define (all_even L)
     (cond    ((null? L) #T)
              ((= (remainder (car L) 2) 1) #F)
              (else (all_even (cdr L)))))
```

5.4.2.3. List-Building Functions

Some functions return not an atom but a list. These functions usually return a simple list (such as the empty list or a singleton list) in the base case; in the recursive case, they use cons or a similar list-construction function to build the overall output list out of a smaller list returned by the recursive function call.

Example: Finding the even numbers in a list

As an example, consider a function (even_list L) which returns a list containing all the even numbers in L. As before, we will assume that L is a list containing only numbers, with no nested lists. For example, (even_list '(8 3 5 4)) should return (8 4).

The empty list will again be the base case, but this time it will return the empty list.

There are two non-empty, recursive cases: a list beginning with an even number, and a list beginning with an odd number. If L begins with an even number, then the first number in L should be included in the list that the function returns; if L begins with an odd number, then that first number should not be included in the return list. In both cases, all of the even numbers in the cdr of L should be included in the return list. This gives us the following function:

```
(define (even_list L)
     (cond    ((null? L) '( ))
              ((= (remainder (car L) 2) 0)
                  (cons (car L) (even_list (cdr L))))
              (else (even_list (cdr L)))))
```

5.4.2.4. Working with nested lists

Some problems require searching through nested lists, and these functions often use two or more recursive calls in the recursive case.

Example: Flattening a list

One example is the problem of flattening a list. We will define a function (flatten L), which returns a list of all the atoms in list L, in the order they occur in L. For example, (flatten '(a (b c) (d))) will return (a b c d), and (flatten '((a b) (c (b a) ((c)))) will return (a b c b a c).

The base case for this function will be the empty list, and the function will return the empty list in this case. There are two recursive cases: the case where the first element is a list, and the case where the first element is an atom. If the first element is itself a list, then it needs to be flattened: we will flatten the car, flatten the cdr, and then append the two lists together to construct the overall output list. On the other hand, if the first element of the list is an atom, then we can flatten the cdr of the list and cons the car of the list onto it to obtain the output list. This gives us the following definition of flatten:

```
(define (flatten L)
    (cond    ((null? L) '())
             ((list? (car L)) (append (flatten (car L))
                                      (flatten (cdr L))))
             (else (cons (car L)
                         (flatten (cdr L)))))))
```

5.4.2.5. Numeric functions

Recursion can also be used to define functions that take one or more numbers as arguments and return a number as a result. For these functions, the base case is usually a small number, such as 0 or 1, and in the recursive case, the return value for N is computed by calling the function recursively on a smaller value of N, such as $N - 1$ or $N/2$.

Example: Factorial

One classic example of a numeric function that is easy to define recursively is the *factorial* function, written $N!$. $N!$ is defined (without recursion) as follows:

$$N! = N * (N - 1) * (N - 2) * \cdots * 1$$

For example, $4! = 4 * 3 * 2 * 1 = 24$. The factorial function can be defined recursively by observing that

$$N = N * (N - 1)!$$

since $(N - 1)! = (N - 1) * (N - 2) * \cdots * 1$. To complete the recursive definition, we add $0! = 1$ as a base case. Scheme notation requires prefix notation, so instead of writing !, we will call the function factorial with one argument; some sample calls are (factorial 3), which returns 6, and (factorial 5), which returns 120. With this notation in place, the Scheme implementation of the recursive factorial algorithm is:

```
(define (factorial N)                    ; Precondition: N >= 0
    (cond    ((= N 0) 1)
             (else (* N (factorial (- N 1)))))))
```

Exercises: Writing functions using recursion

1. Write a Scheme function (sum_positive L) which returns the sum of all the positive numbers in L. Assume that L contains only numbers, with no nested lists. For example, (sum_positive '(-3 8 10 0 -2)) should return 18.

2. Variation: Write a Scheme function (sum_positive L) which returns the sum of all the positive numbers in L. Assume that L contains no nested lists, but that L may contain some non-numbers; ignore any non-numbers in L. For example, (sum_positive '(-3 apple 8 banana 10 0 -2)) should return 18.

3. Another variation: Write a Scheme function (sum_positive L) which returns the sum of all the positive numbers in L. Assume that L contains only numbers, but that L may contain nested lists. For example, (sum_positive '(-3 (8 10) ((0) -2))) should return 18.

4. Write a Scheme function (pos_list L) which returns a list of all the positive numbers in L. Assume that L contains only numbers, with no nested lists. For example, (pos_list '(-3 8 10 0 -2)) should return (8 10).

5. Write a Scheme function (ab L) which returns #T if L contains an *a* followed directly by a *b*, and returns #F otherwise. Assume that L contains no nested lists. For example, (ab '(c a b d a)) should return #T, and (ab '(c b d a c b)) should return #F.

6. Write a Scheme function (nums LB UB) which generates and returns the list of integers starting at lower bound LB and going up through upper bound UB; for example, (nums 3 6) should return (3 4 5 6), and (nums 1 10) should return (1 2 3 4 5 6 7 8 9 10).

7. Write a Scheme function (delete_all Item L) which returns the result of deleting all occurrences of Item from list L. If Item does not appear in L, then delete_all should return L unchanged.

5.5. Programs containing more than one function

Most programmers are familiar with the *divide and conquer* approach to problem-solving, in which:

- A large problem is divided into smaller pieces.

- An algorithm is constructed and a code segment is written for each of the pieces of the problem. Often, each code segment becomes a separate function or procedure.

- The individual code segments are combined into a single program to solve the over-all problem.

This approach is even more useful in functional programming than it is in imperative programming, because of the crucial role played by functions. In fact, the syntax and philosophy of

Scheme force the programmer to break an algorithm into small pieces, each piece of which is coded as a separate functions. This will be illustrated in some examples below.

Two of the coding differences between Scheme and the imperative languages sometimes confuse new Scheme programmers at first:

1)   Scheme uses functions more heavily than do the imperative languages. In general, any segment of an algorithm that uses repetition will require a separate function in Scheme, and in many cases a segment that use a conditional branch will also become a separate function.

2)   In imperative languages, a sequence of operations ("Do X, then do Y") is usually implemented by a code sequence — the code for X, followed by the code for Y. In Scheme, by contrast, a sequence of operations is usually implemented by nested function calls: To accomplish "Do X, then do Y", function Y calls function X.

To illustrate the process of developing a Scheme program that involves writing more than one function, we will look at two examples: Insertion sort, and finding primes using the Sieve of Eratosthenes.

Example: Insertion sort

One standard algorithm for sorting a list of numbers (that is, putting the list of numbers in order from smallest to largest) is insertion sort. In insertion sort, the list is conceptually divided into a sorted part (initially empty) and an unsorted part (initially the entire list). One by one, one item in the unsorted part is removed and inserted into its position in the sorted part. This shrinks the unsorted part by one item. When the unsorted part is empty, then all the items have been sorted, and the algorithm is done.

Here is one sample computation. In our implementation, we will be removing the right-most item from the unsorted part and inserting it into the sorted part at each step, since this how the operations will be carried out when we write the function recursively.

Unsorted part	Sorted part
(5 2 8 9 4)	( )
(5 2 8 9)	(4)
(5 2 8)	(4 9)
(5 2)	(4 8 9)
(5)	(2 4 8 9)
( )	(2 4 5 8 9)

Written recursively, the insertion sort algorithm on list L is:

If list L is empty or a singleton list, return L (since L is already sorted).

Otherwise,

Sort `(cdr L)`, using insertion sort.

Insert `(car L)` into the sorted version of `(cdr L)`, and return the result.

To implement this algorithm, we need to write function `(insert Item L)`, which inserts `Item` into its place in sorted list L. Written recursively, the algorithm for `insert` is:

If L is empty, return the singleton list containing Item.

Else if Item is less than or equal to `(car L)`, then put `Item` onto the front of L and return the result.

Else:

> Insert Item into `(cdr L)`.

> Put `(car L)` onto the front of the previous list and return the result.

Translated into Scheme, this becomes:

```
(define (insertion_sort L)
    ; Return a sorted version of L, using insertion sort
    (cond    ((null? L) L)
             ((null? (cdr L)) L)
             (else (insert (car L) (insertion_sort (cdr L))))))

(define (insert Item L)
    ; Insert Item into its place in sorted list L
    (cond    ((null? L) (list Item))
             ((<= Item (car L)) (cons Item L))
             (else (cons (car L) (insert Item (cdr L)))))
```

Example: Finding prime numbers

The Sieve of Eratosthenes is an algorithm for finding all the prime numbers within a given range (for example, all the prime numbers between 1 and 100). In this example, we will implement this algorithm in Scheme to produce a program which, given an integer N, returns a list of all the prime numbers between 1 and N. The top-level function will be called `primes`, with one integer argument N; `(primes N)` will return a list of all the primes less than or equal to N. Some sample calls to `primes` are:

```
(primes 10)      returns    (2 3 5 7)
(primes 40)      returns    (2 3 5 7 11 13 17 19 23 29 31 37)
```

The basic algorithm is:

1. Generate the list of integers 2..N.
2. Replace all the multiples of the first element in the list by "x".
3. Repeat with the second element in the list, then third, etc.
4. The resulting list contains only primes and "x"s;
   remove the "x"s and return the resulting list of primes.

Steps 1 and 2 will each become a function. Function (nums LB UB) will generate and return the list of integers starting at lower bound LB and going up through upper bound UB; for example, (nums 3 6) will return (3 4 5 6), and (nums 1 10) will return (1 2 3 4 5 6 7 8 9 10). Function (xout N L) performs step 2, replacing every Nth number in L by an x, with the first number in L counted as 1. For example, (xout 3 '(4 5 6 7 8 9 10)) will return (4 5 x 7 8 x 10). The repetition in Step 3 will be accomplished with the recursion in function xout. Step 4 is performed by function sieve. Function sieve looks at the first number in its list argument NumList and deletes its multiples from the cdr of Num-List. (If the first element of NumList is x, the x is discarded.) Function sieve then calls itself recursively to repeat the process on the remainder of the list.

The top-level function (primes N) calls a helping function sieve. Function sieve begins with a list of numbers, NumList, which initially contains the numbers 2..N for some N; as the algorithm progresses, some numbers in the list will be replaced by x, as they are discovered to be composite. These x elements are removed from the list later, as sieve proceeds through its recursive calls. At the end, sieve returns a list of primes, which is then also returned by primes.

These pieces can now be combined into a complete program:

```
; Find all the primes less than or equal to N, using the Sieve of
; Eratosthenes

; Algorithm:
;     Generate the list of integers 2..N
;     Replace all the multiples of the first element in the list by
;         "x".
;     Repeat with the second element in the list, then third, etc.
;     The resulting list contains only primes and "x"s;
;         remove the "x"s and return the resulting list of primes.

(define (primes N)
    ; Return a list of all the primes <= N

    (sieve (nums 2 N)))

(define (sieve NumList)
    ; Return all the primes in NumList, using the Sieve of
    ;         Eratosthenes.
    ; NumList is a list of consecutive integers (initially 2..Max
    ;         for some Max).

    (cond    ((null? NumList) '( ))
             ((eq? (car NumList) 'x)
                 (sieve (cdr NumList)))
             (else
                 (cons    (car NumList)
                          (sieve (xout (car NumList) (cdr NumList)))))))

(define (xout N L)
    ; Replace every Nth number in L by an x.

    (cond    ((null? L) '( ))
             ((eq? (car L) 'x)
                 (cons 'x (xout N (cdr L))))
```

```
          ((= (remainder (car L) N) 0)
              (cons 'x (xout N (cdr L))))
          (else
              (cons (car L) (xout N (cdr L)))))))

(define (nums LB UB)
    ; Return a list of numbers (LB LB+1 LB+2 ... UB)
    ; E.g., (nums 2 5) returns (2 3 4 5)

    (cond    ((> LB UB) '( ))
             (else (cons LB (nums (+ LB 1) UB)))))
```

Exercises: Writing multiple functions

1. Change function `insertion_sort` so that it sorts in descending order instead of
    ascending order. For example, as revised, `(insertion_sort '(3 6 7 2 3 8))`
    should return `(8 7 6 3 3 2)`. (ins, desc)

2. Write a function `(mode L)` which returns the mode of list L (that is, the most commonly
    occurring item in list L). For example, `(mode '(4 5 1 3 8 5 8 5 6))` should
    return 5. If there is more than one mode, your function may return any of the modes. For
    example, `(mode '(4 5 1 4 1))` could return either 4 or 1.

    Suggestions: The easiest way to find the mode of a list is to sort the list, then look for the
    longest sequence of consecutive identical numbers.

    In addition to function `mode`, define a function `(most_common L)`, which returns the
    mode of *sorted* list L; and define a function `(longest_sequence L Curr_Item
    Curr_Count Mode Mode_Count)`, which returns the mode of sorted list L, given
    that:

    > Mode is the most common item found so far,

    > `Mode_Count` is the number of times `Mode` occurs,

    > `Curr_Item` is the item in the current sequence in the list, and

    > `Curr_Count` is the number of times `Curr_Item` has been seen so far.

    Function `insertion_sort` will, of course, also be useful.

Chapter 6: Data Structures

Scheme lists can be used to implement a variety of data structures. To illustrate, this chapter will show Scheme implementations of a stack and a tree.

6.1. Implementing a stack

A stack is an abstract data type that stores a sequence of items, usually visualized as a vertical pile of objects; items can be added to or removed from the top of the stack, but the middle of the stack cannot be viewed or modified. The operations on a stack, stated in Scheme form, are:

(push Item S)
> Place Item on the top of stack S, and return the resulting stack.

(pop S)
> Remove the top item from stack S, and return the resulting stack.

(top S)
> Return the top item of stack S. Stack S is not changed by this operation.

(empty? S)
> Return #T if stack S is empty, and #F otherwise. Stack S is not changed by this operation.

The most natural way to store a stack is as a list. Since the front of the list is the end most easily accessed with operations *car*, *cdr*, and *cons*, the front of the list will be designated as the top of the stack. Thus, stack

> a
> b
> c

will be represented by list (a b c). Popping the stack produces stack

> b
> c

represented as list (b c); pushing d onto this new stack produces

> d
> b
> c

represented as list (d b c). An empty stack is represented as an empty list.

Implementing these stack operations turns out to be quite simple. To push an item onto the stack, cons the item onto the beginning of the list. To pop the stack, take the cdr of the stack. To view the top of the stack, take the car of the stack. And null? checks whether a list is empty.

Thus, it turns out that all four operations can be implemented by simply renaming existing operations. Not only will the function definitions be short, they can be done using the first form of define:

```
(define push cons)
(define pop cdr)
(define top car)
(define empty? null?)
```

Sequences of stack operations turn into nested function calls; for example, the sequence of commands

- pop the stack

- pop the stack

- push d

- push e

starting with stack (a b c), becomes the nest of function calls

```
(push 'e (push 'd (pop (pop '(a b c))))).
```

As an example of a problem which can be solved using a stack, consider the problem of determining whether a string contains balanced parentheses. The parentheses in " (( )) ( ) " are balanced, because every left parenthesis has a matching right parenthesis. But " ( )) " is not balanced, because there are too many right parentheses, and " (( ) " is not balanced, because there are too many left parentheses. ") (" is also not balanced, even though there are the same number of left parentheses as right.

The algorithm for using a stack to detect balanced parentheses is:

> Repeat:
>
> > If you see a left parenthesis, push it onto the stack.
> >
> > If you see a right parenthesis,
> >
> > > If the top of the stack is a left parenthesis, pop the stack
> > >
> > > Else halt and return #F.
>
> until there are no more input characters.
>
> If the stack is empty, return #T
>
> Else return #F.

To implement this in Scheme, we first need some functions for dealing with strings. Scheme contains a large collection of string functions. Most useful for this parenthesis-balancing algorithm is the function string->list, which converts a string to a list of characters; using this function will allow us to use familiar list functions to work with strings of parentheses. As an example, (string->list "(())") returns (#\(#\(#\) #\)). Since #\(and #\) are rather ugly-looking representations of left and right parenthesis, respectively, we will also write two utility functions:

```
(define (left_par c) (eq? c '#\( ))
(define (right_par c) (eq? c '#\) ))
```

(left_par c) returns #T if c is a left parenthesis character, and (right_par c) returns #T if c is a right parenthesis character.

The top-level function is (balanced Str), which returns #T if string Str is a string of balanced parentheses, and returns #F otherwise. It calls string->list to convert the string to a list of parenthesis characters, and calls a second function balanced_s with an initially empty stack to perform the check for balanced parenthesis. (balanced_s L S) takes two arguments — a list of parenthesis characters, and a stack — and implements the above algorithm for checking the balance of parentheses. (The s in balanced_s stands for *stack*, as a reminder that balanced_s uses a stack for its calculations.

```
(define (balanced Str)
    ; Return #T if string Str is a string of balanced parentheses,
    ; and #F otherwise.
    (balanced_s (string->list Str) '()))

(define (balanced_s L S)
    ; Determine if list L is a list of balanced parentheses,
    ; using (initially empty) stack S.   Return #T or #F.
    (cond    ((null? L) (empty? S))
        ((left_par (car L))
            (balanced_s (cdr L) (push (car L) S)))
        ((and (right_par (car L)) (empty? S)) #F)
        ((and (right_par (car L)) (left_par (top S)))
            (balanced_s (cdr L) (pop S)))
        (else #F)))

; Predicates to recognize left and right parenthesis characters
(define (left_par c) (eq? c '#\( ))
(define (right_par c) (eq? c '#\) ))


; Stack operations
(define push cons)
(define pop cdr)
(define top car)
(define empty? null?)
```

6.2. Implementing a binary tree

A binary tree can be implemented using nested Scheme lists: the value at the node is the first item in the list, followed by the left subtree of the node, followed by the right subtree of the node. The empty tree is represented by the empty list. For example, the tree

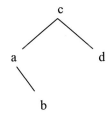

can be represented as `(c (a () (b () ())) (d () ()))`, and the tree

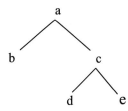

can be represented as `(a (b () ()) (c (d () ()) (e () ())))`.

Binary trees are trees in which each node has at most two children. The first sample tree above is not a binary tree, but the second sample is a binary tree. A binary search tree is a special kind of binary tree in which the nodes are ordered: Every value in the left subtree is less than the value at the root, and every value in the right subtree is less than the value at the root; and this property is true recursively of the left and right subtrees. The exact meaning of "less than" is specified for each particular problem: for numbers, $\leq$ is a natural choice; for characters, alphabetical order is a good choice; and so on. If we take alphabetical order as the node ordering for characters, then

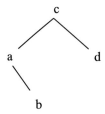

is a binary search tree, but

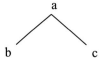

is not a binary search tree, because b > a.

Some typical operations on binary search trees are insertion of a node, deletion of a node, tree traversal, and search for a node in the tree. In this section, we will implement insertion of a node and one method of tree traversal; some other tree operations will be left for exercises.

Both operations will make use of function `(left T)`, which returns the left subtree of tree T, and `(right T)`, which returns the right subtree:

```
(define left cadr)
(define right caddr)
```

6.2.1. Insertion

To insert a value into a binary search tree, we first search through the tree to find the place where the node belongs. Eventually this search will end at an empty subtree below a node with 0 or 1 children. The empty subtree is replaced by a single-node tree containing the new value.

Function (insert Item T) inserts Item into tree T. The algorithm is recursive, with four cases to consider:

1) *Tree T is empty*: A single-node tree containing the new value should be returned.

2) *Item is equal to the value at the root of T*: This means that Item is already in the tree. Since no item should be duplicated in a binary search tree, T is returned unchanged.

3) *Item is less than the value at the root of T*: This means that Item should be in the left subtree. Call insert recursively on the left subtree, and make the tree returned by insert the new left subtree of the overall tree.

4) *Item is greater than the value at the root of T*: This means that Item should be in the right subtree. Call insert recursively on the right subtree, and make the tree returned by insert the new right subtree of the overall tree.

As a Scheme function, this becomes:

```
(define (insert Item T)                          ; Insert Item into BST T
    (cond    ((null? T) (list Item '() '()))     ; Empty tree
             ((equal? Item (car T)) T)           ; Item = root
             ((< Item (car T))                   ; Item < root
                 (list (car T) (insert Item (left T)) (right T)))
             (else                               ; Item > root
                 (list (car T) (left T) (insert Item (right T)))) ))
```

6.2.2. Inorder tree traversal

Traversing a binary tree means systematically visiting each node in the tree, so that each node is visited exactly once. There are three primary tree traversal algorithms: *preorder*, *inorder*, and *postorder*. In this section, we will look at inorder traversal; preorder and postorder traversal will be left as exercises.

For simplicity, in this example we will let "visiting" a node mean inserting its value into a list. For other problems, "visit" can be redefined to be some other operation: adding the node's value into a sum, printing the node's value, or some other task.

To traverse a tree inorder, the nodes are visited in this order:

• Traverse the left subtree inorder.

• Visit the root.

• Traverse the right subtree inorder.

For example, an inorder traversal visits the nodes of this tree

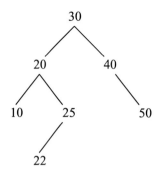

in this order: `10 20 22 25 30 40 50`

Implemented in Scheme, this algorithm becomes:

```
(define (traverse_inorder T)       ; Return a list of nodes in T
    (cond    ((null? T) '( ))
             (else (append    (traverse_inorder (left T))
                       (cons    (car T)
                       (traverse_inorder (right T)))))))
```

Exercises: Data structures

1. Change function `balanced_s` so that it permits extra characters to appear in the string of parentheses. These extra characters should be ignored when determining whether the parentheses are balanced. For example, with the new definition of `balanced_s`, `(bal-anced "(a())b(c)d")` should return #T, and `(balanced "(a()")` should return #F.

2. *Preorder traversal* visits nodes in the following order:

    •   Visit the root.

    •   Traverse the left subtree inorder.

    •   Traverse the right subtree inorder.

    For example, a preorder traversal visits the nodes of this tree

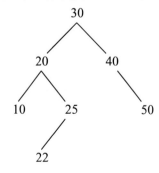

in this order: `30 20 10 25 22 40 50`. Write a Scheme function which performs preorder traversal and returns a list of the nodes in the tree in the order that they are visited.

3. *Postorder traversal* visits nodes in the following order:

- Traverse the left subtree inorder.

- Traverse the right subtree inorder.

- Visit the root.

For example, a postorder traversal visits the nodes of this tree

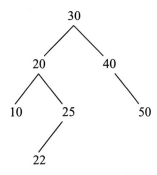

in this order: 10 22 25 20 30 50 40. Write a Scheme function which performs postorder traversal and returns a list of the nodes in the tree in the order that they are visited.

4. Change function `traverse_inorder` so that instead of inserting the nodes' values into a list, it adds them into a sum; the revised `traverse_inorder` should return the sum of the values of the nodes in the tree. For example, `(traverse_inorder '(5 (2 () ()) (7 () (10 () ()))))` should return 24.

Chapter 7: Programming Projects

This chapter lists a number of medium-sized programming projects, for further practice in applying Scheme to new problems. The solution to most of these problems is about a page long; the problems are large enough to give some real programming practice, but small enough that they can be solved using the subset of Scheme presented in this book. For most of the problems, only the top-level function has been described in detail; feel free to define any additional functions needed to solve the problems.

1. Printer Queues

Write a program to simulate a pair of printer queues. There are two printers, each with its own queue. Each job has a name (represented as a single letter) and a duration (represented as a positive integer). When a new job arrives, it is added to the end of the printer queue that is currently "shortest", where the length of a queue is the sum of the durations of the jobs in the queue. If the two queues are exactly the same length, add the new job to queue 1. In this simulation, you will only be adding jobs to the queues; no jobs will leave the queues in this problem. The input is the list of jobs to be added to the queues. The output is the contents of the two queues that result.

Example:

Jobs (a 10), (b 5), (c 3), (d 4), and (e 6) arrive, in that order.

Job (a 10) is added to queue 1. Since queue 2 is now shorter, (b 5) is added to queue 2. Queue 2 is still shorter, so (c 3) is added to queue 2. (d 4) is also added to queue 2. At this point, queue 1 has length 10 and queue 2 has length $5 + 3 + 4 = 12$, so (e 6) is added to queue 1.

The final states of the queues are:

Queue 1: (a 10), (e 6)

Queue 2: (b 5), (c 3), (d 4)

To implement this in Scheme, define a function (queues L) which takes a list of jobs L as a parameter and returns a 2-element list containing the 2 resulting printer queues.

For example, (queues '((a 10) (b 5) (c 3) (d 4) (e 6))) should return (((a 10) (e 6)) ((b 5) (c 3) (d 4))).

I recommend breaking the problem down in the following way:

a) Function (queues2 Jobs Q1 Q2) returns the result of adding all the jobs in the list Jobs to the pair of queues Q1 and Q2. queues can call queues2 with a pair of initially empty queues.

b) Function (add_to_end Item L) returns the result of adding Item to the end of list L.

c) Function (qlength Q) returns the length of queue Q, where the length is the sum of the durations of the jobs in Q. For example, (qlength '((a 2) (b 3) (c 20))) should return 25.

2. Word frequency count

Write a program which, given a sequence of words, will produce a frequency list that contains each word found in the input followed by the number of times that word appeared in the input. For example, for

```
the red box is on the blue box and the green box
```

we have this frequency count:

```
the     3
red     1
box     3
is      1
on      1
blue    1
and     1
green   1
```

To implement this in Scheme, write a Scheme function `(frequency_list WordList)` which returns a list of pairs representing each word in WordList and the number of times that word occurs in WordList. In each pair, the first item in the list is a word, and the second item is the number of occurrences of that word.

For example, `(frequency_list '(the red box is on the blue box and the green box)` should return `((the 3) (red 1) (box 3) (is 1) (on 1) (blue 1) (and 1) (green 1))`.

The words in the input may occur in any order in the frequency list; for example, `((green 1) (and 1) (blue 1) (on 1) (is 1) (box 3) (red 1) (the 3))` is an equally good solution. No word should be repeated in the frequency list, however: `((green 1) (and 1) (blue 1) (on 1) (is 1) (box 1) (box 2) (red 1) (the 1) (the 1) (the 1))` is not an acceptable solution.

2.1. Variation: Sorted List

Write a Scheme program to solve the frequency list problem, but return a frequency list that is sorted in descending order by number of occurrences, so that the most frequent words occur at the beginning of the list and the least frequent at the end. Words of equal frequency may be listed in any order.

For example, `(sorted_frequency_list '(the red box is on the blue box and the green box)` should return `((the 3) (box 3) (red 1) (is 1) (on 1) (blue 1) (and 1) (green 1))`.

2.2. Variation: Most Common Word

Write a Scheme program which, given a list of words, returns the most frequently occurring word in the list. (In case of a tie, any of the most-frequently-occurring words may be returned.)

For example, `(most_frequent '(the red box is on the blue box and the green box)` should return `the`. Returning `box` would be an equally correct solution.

3. Flower garden

Hilda is planting her flower garden, and she wants to find an arrangement of flowers that she thinks will look pretty. The flowers will be planted in one straight line. She has two criteria for the flower arrangement:

1) No two flowers of the same color may be next to each other.

2) The height of each flower must be no more than 2 inches different from the heights of its immediate neighbors.

One example of an acceptable flower arrangement is (numbers indicate inches in height):

Iris	Lily	Canna	Canna	Lily
Purple	White	Orange	Yellow	Orange
36	34	36	36	37

This arrangement is also acceptable:

Petunia	Tulip	Marigold	Crocus
Pink	Red	Yellow	Purple
12	10	8	6

This is a third acceptable arrangement:

Pansy	Tulip	Crocus	Crocus
Purple	Red	White	Purple
7	8	6	6

The next arrangement is not acceptable, because it places an orange canna next to an orange lily:

Iris	Lily	Canna	Lily	Canna
Purple	White	Orange	Orange	Yellow
36	34	36	36	37

The next arrangement is unacceptable, because a marigold that is 8 inches high is next to a lily that is 34 inches high:

Petunia	Tulip	Marigold	Lily
Pink	Red	Yellow	White
12	10	8	34

Finally, the next arrangement is unacceptable due to both color and height -- a yellow tulip is next to a yellow marigold, and a 9-inch-tall marigold is next to a 6-inch-tall crocus.

Petunia	Tulip	Marigold	Crocus
Pink	Yellow	Yellow	Purple
12	10	9	6

The input to the program will be a list of triples specifying the name, color, and height in inches of each flower. When the program is run, it should tell the user whether this list describes an acceptable flower arrangement.

To implement this in Scheme, write a function (`flowers FlowerList`), which returns #T if `FlowerList` describes an acceptable flower arrangement, and returns #F otherwise. `FlowerList` is a list of flower data: for each flower, `FlowerList` will contain a list with 3 items: a flower name, a color, and a height. (You may assume that `FlowerList` will be in this format; you do not have to do any format-related error-checking.)

Examples:

(flowers '((petunia pink 12) (tulip red 10) (marigold yellow 8) (crocus purple 6))) should return #T

(flowers '((petunia pink 12) (tulip yellow 10) (marigold yellow 9) (crocus purple 6))) should return #F

4. Feuding Diners

You are responsible for the seating arrangements at a dinner party. All the guests will be seated around a large circular table. Unfortunately, you must take several family feuds into account in your seat assignments:

- The Smith family and the Jones family are in the midst of a feud: No one named Smith can sit next to anyone named Jones.

- The Smith family is also feuding with the Baker family: No one named Smith can sit next to anyone named Baker.

- Further, the Baker family is feuding with the Brown family: No one named Baker can sit next to anyone named Brown.

The input to your program will be a list of first and last names representing a proposed seating arrangement. (Because the table is circular, consider the first name in the list to be adjacent to the last name in the list.) Your program must inform the user whether the proposed seating arrangement is a permissible one, given the collection of family feuds.

Examples:

Violet Brown, Roger Baker, Wilbur Hamilton, Mildred Jones, Alfred Jones: This is not a legal seating arrangement, because Violet Brown is seated next to Roger Baker.

Mary Smith, Ingrid Baker, Mildred Jones, Alfred Jones: This is not a legal seating arrangement, because Mary Smith is seated next to Alfred Jones.

Thaddeus Baker, Phyllis Andrews, Frieda Jones, Hortense Williams, Josiah Smith, Annabelle McKay: This is a legal seating arrangement.

To solve this problem in Scheme, define a function (`seats_ok L`) which takes a list of names L as a parameter and returns #T if the seating arrangement in L is acceptable, and #F if it is unacceptable. Each name in list L will be a 2-element list containing the person's first name and last name. You may assume that list L will be in the correct format when the function is called; you do not have to error-check for a non-list or an incorrectly formed list. In your program, you may write and call any additional functions that are helpful in the computation.

For example, (seats_ok '((Mary Smith) (Ingrid Baker) (Mildred Jones) (Alfred Jones))) should return #F, and (seats_ok '((Thaddeus Baker) (Phyllis Andrews))) should return #T.

5. Properties of relations

A relation over a set S is a set of ordered pairs of elements of S. A set can be represented in Scheme as a list, and a relation can be represented as a list of pairs. For example, if set S is (a b c d), then ((a b) (c d) (b b) (a c)) specifies that a is related to b, c is related to d, b is related to itself, and a is related to c. Notice that while the pairs are ordered, the set is not: ((a b) (a c)) is the same relation as ((a c) (a b)), but ((a b) (a c)) and ((a b) (c a)) are different relations. Relations can have a number of different properties:

- A relation over set S is **reflexive** if every element in S is related to itself. For example, if set S is (a b c), then ((a a) (b a) (b b) (c c) (c a)) is reflexive, because a is related to a, b is related to b, and c is related to c. ((a a) (b c) (c c)) is not reflexive, because b is not related to b.

- A relation over set S is **symmetric** if this property holds: for every $x, y \in S$, if x is related to y, then y is related to x. For example, if set S is (a b c), then ((a b) (b a) (b b) (a c) (c a)) is symmetric, but ((a b) (b b) (a c) (c a)) is not symmetric.

- A relation over set S is **antisymmetric** if this property holds: for every $x, y \in S$, with $x \neq y$, if x is related to y, then y is not related to x. For example, if set S is (a b c), then ((a b) (b b) (a c)) is antisymmetric, but ((a b) (b b) (a c) (c a)) is not antisymmetric. Note that it is possible for a relation to be neither symmetric nor antisymmetric: if set S is (a b c), then ((a b) (b b) (a c) (c a)) is neither symmetric nor antisymmetric.

- A relation over set S is **transitive** if this property holds: for every $x, y\ z \in S$, if x is related to y, and y is related to z, then x is related to z. For example, if set S is (a b c), then ((a b) (b b) (b c) (a c)) is transitive, but ((a b) (b b) (b c)) is not transitive.

- A relation over set S is an **equivalence relation** if it is reflexive, symmetric, and transitive. For example, if set S is (a b c), then ((a a) (a b) (a c) (b a) (b b) (b c) (c a) (c b) (c c)) is an equivalence relation.

- A relation over set S is a **partial order** if it is reflexive, antisymmetric, and transitive. For example, if set S is (a b c d), then ((a b) (a c) (c d) (a d) (a a) (b b) (c c)) is a partial order.

Write Scheme predicates to check each of these properties:

a) Function (reflexive? Set Relation) should return #T if the given Relation over the given Set is reflexive and should return #F otherwise. For example, (reflexive? '(a b c) '((a a) (b a) (b b) (c c) (c a))) should return #T, and (reflexive? '(a b c) '((a a) (b c) (c c))) should return #F.

b) Function (symmetric? Set Relation) should return #T if the given Relation over the given Set is symmetric and should return #F otherwise. For example, (symmetric? '(a b c) '((a b) (b a) (b b) (a c) (c a))) should return #T, and (symmetric? '(a b c) '((a b) (b b) (a c) (c a))) should return #F.

c) Function (antisymmetric? Set Relation) should return #T if the given Relation over the given Set is antisymmetric and should return #F otherwise. For example,

(antisymmetric? '(a b c) '((a b) (b b) (a c))) should return #T,
and (antisymmetric? '(a b c) '((a b) (b b) (a c) (c a))) should
return #F.

d) Function (transitive? Set Relation) should return #T if the given Relation
over the given Set is transitive and should return #F otherwise. For example, (transitive? '(a b c) '((a b) (b b) (b c) (a c))) should return #T, and
(transitive? '(a b c) '((a b) (b b) (b c))) should return #F.

e) Function (equivalence_relation? Set Relation) should return #T if the
given Relation over the given Set is an equivalence relation and should return #F otherwise. For example, (equivalence_relation? '(a b c) '((a b) (b c)
(a c) (a a) (b b) (c c)) should return #T, and (equivalence_relation? '(a b c) '((a b) (b c) (a a) (b b)) should return #F.

f) Function (partial_order? Set Relation) should return #T if the given Relation over the given Set is a partial_order and should return #F otherwise. For example,
(partial_order? '(a b c) '((a b) (a c) (c d) (a d) (a a) (b
b) (c c))) should return #T, and (partial_order? '(a b c) '((a b) (a
c) (c d) (b b) (c c))) should return #F.

You may assume that the parameters will contain well-formed data when the function is called:
Set will contain a list of elements, and Relation will contain a list of pairs of elements of
Set.

6. Reflexive Transitive Closure

The **reflexive transitive closure** of a relation **R** is the smallest relation that includes all the
pairs in **R** and is both reflexive and transitive. (For definitions of terminology about relations, see
the previous problem.) For example, if R1 is a relation over the set (a b c d), and R1 is the
relation

((a b) (b c) (c d) (c c)),

then the reflexive transitive closure of R1 is the relation

((a b) (b c) (c d) (c c) (a a) (b b) (d d) (a c) (b d) (a d)).

As another example, if R2 is a relation over (a b c), and R2 is the relation

((a a) (b b) (b a) (a c)),

then the reflexive transitive closure of R2 is the relation

((a a) (b b) (b a) (a c) (c c) (b c)).

Note that if a relation is already reflexive and transitive, then the the reflexive transitive closure of
that relation will simply be the relation itself. For example, if R3 is a relation over (a b c),
and R3 is the relation

((a a) (b b) (c c) (c a) (a c)),

then the reflexive transitive closure of R3 is R3 itself.

Write a function (rt_closure Set Relation) which returns the reflexive transitive closure of Relation, assuming that Relation is a relation over the given Set. For
example, (rt_closure '(a b c) '((a a) (b b) (b a) (a c))) should return
((a a) (b b) (b a) (a c) (c c) (b c)).

Hint: Use this approach:

> Add the pairs needed to make the relation reflexive.
>
> Repeat:
>
> > For each (*x y*), (*y z*) in the relation, if (*x z*) is not in the relation, then add (*x z*) to a list of new pairs.
> >
> > Add all the new pairs to the relation.
>
> until one pass through all the pairs in the relation produces no new pairs.

Example:

> Original relation: ((a b) (b c) (c d) (c c))
>
> Add pairs to make relation reflexive: ((a b) (b c) (c d) (c c) (a a) (b b) (d d))
>
> Make relation transitive:
>
> > *First pass*: New pairs are (a c) and (b d).
> >
> > > *Add new pairs:* ((a b) (b c) (c d) (c c) (a a) (b b) (d d) (a c) (b d))
> >
> > *Second pass*: New pair is (a d)
> >
> > > *Add new pair:* ((a b) (b c) (c d) (c c) (a a) (b b) (d d) (a c) (b d) (a d))
> >
> > *Third pass*: No new pairs
>
> Result: ((a b) (b c) (c d) (c c) (a a) (b b) (d d) (a c) (b d) (a d))

7. Checking Correct Dates

A date can be specified as a list containing a month, a day, and a year. Months can be represented as numbers in the range 1-12, as symbols for the month names (January-December), or as symbols for abbreviated month names (Jan, Feb, Mar, Apr, May, Jun, Jul, Aug, Sept, Oct, Nov, Dec). The date elements can be specified in the order (*Month Day Year*) or in the order (*Day Month Year*). To avoid ambiguity, any date in which the month is a number will be specified as (*Month Day Year*). Also to avoid ambiguity, all years will be represented as full integers, not two-digit abbreviations: 1987, not 87. All of these lists represent dates:

```
(Jan 1 2001)
(July 4 1776)
(25 December 1961)
(6 23 1912)
```

Write a function (valid_date Date) which returns #T if Date is a valid date, and #F otherwise. To check the validity of the date, you must check:

- whether Date is, in fact, a list of length 3
- whether the month, if a name, is a correct month name
- whether the month, if a number, is in the range 1-12

- whether the day and year are numbers
- whether the day is in the proper range for the month. January, March, May, July, August, October, and December have 31 days; April, June, September, and November have 30 days; and February has 28 or 29 days, depending on whether the year is a leap year. A year is a leap year if it is divisible by 400, or if it is divisible by 4 but not 100.

Because the current Gregorian calendar system was adopted in Great Britain and the American colonies on September 2, 1752, and different systems were followed before this date, for simplicity we will consider only dates after September 2, 1752, to be valid dates. Thus, valid_date should return #F for any date prior to September 2, 1752.

Examples:
```
(valid_date '(Jan 1 2001)) should return #T.
(valid_date '(July 4 1776)) should return #T.
(valid_date '(25 December 1961)) should return #T.
(valid_date '(6 23 1912)) should return #T.
(valid_date '(1 2 3 4 5)) should return #F.
(valid_date '(a b c)) should return #F.
(valid_date '(FakeMonth 1 1700)) should return #F.
(valid_date '(April 31 1802)) should return #F.
(valid_date '(January 45 1965)) should return #F.
(valid_date '(23 6 1912)) should return #F.
(valid_date '(February 29 2000)) should return #T.
(valid_date '(February 29 1800)) should return #F.
(valid_date '(March 4 1374)) should return #F.
```

8. Past, Present, and Future

Write a function (when Date Now) whose two arguments, Date and Now, are both dates, represented using the range of formats described in the previous problem. Assuming Now is today's date, (when Date Now) should return

past
> if Date is earlier than Now

present
> if Date represents the same date as Now

future
> if Date is later than Now

invalid
> if either Date or Now is an invalid date.

Examples:
```
(when '(Jan 25 2003) '(July 8 2003)) should return past.
(when '(25 December 2258) '(7 8 2003)) should return future.
(when '(7 8 2003) '(8 July 2003)) should return present.
(when '(April 31 1802) '(8 July 2003)) should return invalid.
```

9. Date distances

Write a function `(days Date Now)` whose two arguments, `Date` and `Now`, are both dates, represented using the range of formats used in the previous problem. Assuming `Now` is today's date, `(when Date Now)` should return the number of days between `Date` and `Now`. If `Date` is before `Now`, the result should be a negative integer; if `Date` is after `Now`, the result should be a positive integer; and if `Date` and `Now` represent the same day, the result should be zero. If either `Date` or `Now` is an invalid date, `days` should return `invalid`.

Examples:

```
(days '(July 1 2003) '(July 8 2003)) should return -7.
(days '(8 July 2004) '(7 8 2003)) should return 366.
(days '(7 8 2003) '(8 July 2003)) should return 0.
(days '(April 31 1802) '(8 July 2003)) should return invalid.
```

10. Hamiltonian circuit

One way to represent a graph in Scheme is to use an adjacency list. The adjacency list contains one entry for each vertex in the graph. Each of these entries contains the name *v* of a vertex, followed by the names of all the vertices that are adjacent to *v*. (More precisely, the list for vertex *v* will contain the names of every vertex *w* such that there is an arc from *v* to *w*.)

For example, the directed graph G_1

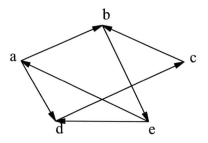

can be represented by the adjacency list

```
(    (a b d)
     (b e)
     (c b)
     (d c)
     (e a d)      ),
```

the directed graph G_2

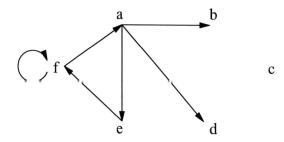

can be represented by the adjacency list

```
(    (a b d e)
     (b)
     (c)
     (d)
     (e f)
     (f a f)        ),
```

and the undirected graph G_3

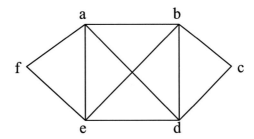

can be represented by the adjacency list

```
(    (a b d e f)
     (b a c d e)
     (c b d)
     (d a b c e)
     (e a b d f)
     (f a e)        ).
```

A **Hamiltonian circuit** in a graph G is a path through the graph that begins and ends at the same vertex and includes every vertex in G exactly once. For example, graph G_1 contains the Hamiltonian circuit (a d c b e a), and graph G_3 contains the Hamiltonian circuits (a b c d e f a) and (a d c b e f a), along with the reversals of these circuits, (a f e d c b a) and (a f e b c d a). Graph G_2 does not contain a Hamiltonian circuit.

Write a function (hamilton Graph) which returns a Hamiltonian circuit through the given Graph. If more than one Hamiltonian circuit exists, the function may return any one of them. Return the atom none if no Hamiltonian circuit exists.

For example, (hamilton '(((a b d) (b e) (c b) (d c) (e a d)))) should return (a d c b e a).

Chapter 8: For Further Reading

This document is not intended as a comprehensive description of the Scheme programming language; rather, it is intended to introduce the functional programming paradigm, with Scheme as one example of this paradigm. With this in mind, I have emphasized the features of Scheme that are most consistent with functional programming. Scheme does contain some features that allow a measure of imperative-style programming; to learn about these features, read one or more of the books below. The books listed here also contain descriptions of the many built-in functions in Scheme, which will be of interest to the reader who wishes to go on and write longer, more sophisticated Scheme programs.

One of the classic Scheme textbooks is Harold Abelson and Gerald Jay Sussman with Julie Sussman, *Structure and Interpretation of Computer Programs*, (MIT Press/McGraw-Hill, 1985). A more gentle text, written for beginning programmers, is Brian Harvey and Matthew Wright, *Simply Scheme* (MIT Press, 1994). Also for beginning programmers is *The Schematics of Computation*, by Vincent S. Manis and James J. Little (Prentice Hall, 1995), which includes an overview of several general computer science topics along with Scheme programming. *The Schemer's Guide*, by Iain Ferguson with Edward Martin and Burt Kaufman (Schemers Inc., 1990) describes Scheme for an audience of middle school and high school readers, but it is entertaining and useful for older readers as well. *The Little Schemer*, by Daniel P. Friedman and Matthias Felleisen (MIT Press, 4th edition, 1996) provides a tutorial introduction to the language.

A good reference book for Scheme is R. Kent Dybvig, *The Scheme Programming Language*, (MIT Press, 3rd edition, 2003). Some interesting practice problems, and a more detailed history of the development of LISP and Scheme, appear in *Programming for Artificial Intelligence*, by Wolfgang Kreutzer and Bruce McKenzie (Addison-Wesley 1991).

The Lambda Calculus and the other computation models listed in chapter 1 are described in James L. Hein, *Theory of Computation: an Introduction* (Jones and Bartlett, 1996). This book also discusses properties of relations and the standard method for computing the reflexive transitive closure of a relation.

There are many good textbooks that describe the stack and tree data structures discussed in chapter 6. One of these is *Data Structures and Program Design in C++*, by Robert L. Kruse and Alexander J. Ryba (Prentice-Hall, 1999).

If you noticed that your solution to the Hamiltonian circuit problem ran very slowly for large graphs, then you may be interested in *Computers and Intractibility: A Guide to the Theory of NP-Completeness* by Michael R. Garey and David S. Johnson (New York: W. H. Freeman, 1979). This book discusses the Hamiltonian circuit problem and a family of related problems, called the NP-Complete problems; all of these problems can be solved, but it is difficult (perhaps impossible) to write a program that solves them quickly.

Scheme and the other dialects of LISP are not the only functional programming languages that have been developed. Others include ML (Milner, Tofte, Harper, and MacQueen, *The Definition of Standard ML*, MIT Press, 1997; Ullman, *Elements of ML Programming, ML97 Edition*, Prentice-Hall, 1997) and Haskell (Thompson, *Haskell: The Craft of Functional Programming*, Addison-Wesley, 1996); both of these languages differ from LISP and Scheme in providing strong typing and type declarations.

Appendix 1: Answers to Exercises

Chapter 1

Scheme notation

1a. $\sqrt{x} + 5$

1b. $(x - y) * (z + 2)$

1c. $\dfrac{10}{((x + 1) - y)}$

1d. $\sqrt{2x}$

1e. $\left| \dfrac{y + 2}{x - 1} \right|$

2a. (* 5 (+ x y))

2b. (- (* x y) (* x z))

2c. (/ (* 2 x) 3)

2d. (/ (* 10 (+ x 5)) (- y 1))

2e. (sqrt (- (* 16 x) (* 3 y)))

Chapter 2

Identifiers and constants

1. *b*, *c*, and *e* are legal identifiers. *a* and *d* are not, because an identifier cannot start with a character that can begin a number; *a* begins with a digit, and *d* begins with a – character.

2a. string

2b. number

2c. symbol

2d. not a legal constant

2e. symbol

2f. number

Chapter 3

Car, Cdr, and Cons

1. lion

2. ((tiger cheetah) leopard)

3. (bear fox)

4. ((wolf))

5. (giraffe)

6. gorilla

7. (lion bobcat)

8. antelope

9. (zebra)

10. (fox bear rabbit)

11. ((lion tiger) giraffe antelope)

12. lion

13. (tiger)

14. (squirrel fox rabbit)

15. (lion giraffe zebra)

16. (car (cdr '(a b (c (d) e)))), or (cadr '(a b (c (d) e)))

17. (car (cdr (cdr (car (cdr (cdr '(a b (c (d) e)))))))))

18. (car (car (cdr (car (cdr (cdr '(a b (c (d) e)))))))))

Chapter 4

List Implementation

1. (cons 'a (cons 'b '( )))

2.

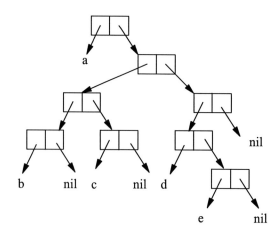

3.

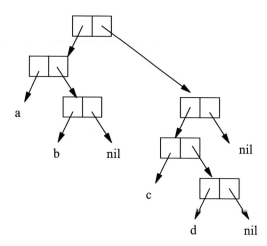

4. ((a b c) d)

5.   (a b (c))

Chapter 5

Writing simple functions

1.   (define (tri_area base height) (* 0.5 base height))

2.   (define (avg4 w x y z) (/ (+ w x y z) 4))

Writing functions using cond

1.   (define (how_big N)
            (cond ((not (number? N)) "not a number")
                  ((<= N 10) "small")
                  ((and (> N 10) (<= N 20)) "medium")
                  ((and (> N 20) (< N 100)) "big")
                  (else "very big")))

2.   (define (tax income status)
            (cond ((and (<= income 50000) (eq? status 's)) (* income 0.15))
                  ((and (> income 50000) (eq? status 's)) (* income 0.25))
                  ((and (<= income 50000) (eq? status 'm)) (* income 0.10))
                  (else (* income 0.20))))

Writing functions using recursion

1.   (define (sum_positive L)
            (cond ((null? L) 0)
                  ((> (car L) 0) (+ (car L) (sum_positive (cdr L))))
                  (else (sum_positive (cdr L)))))

2.   (define (sum_positive L)
            (cond ((null? L) 0)
                  ((not (number? (car L))) (sum_positive (cdr L)))
                  ((> (car L) 0) (+ (car L) (sum_positive (cdr L))))
                  (else (sum_positive (cdr L)))))

3.   (define (sum_positive L)
            (cond ((null? L) 0)
                  ((list? (car L))
                        (+ (sum_positive (car L)) (sum_positive (cdr L))))
                  ((> (car L) 0) (+ (car L) (sum_positive (cdr L))))
                  (else (sum_positive (cdr L)))))

4.   (define (pos_list L)
            (cond ((null? L) '())
                  ((> (car L) 0) (cons (car L) (pos_list (cdr L))))
                  (else (pos_list (cdr L)))))

5.   (define (ab L)
           (cond ((null? L) #F)
                 ((null? (cdr L)) #F)
                 ((and (eq? (car L) 'a) (eq? (cadr L) 'b)) #T)
                 (else (ab (cdr L)))))

6.   (define (nums LB UB)
           (cond ((> LB UB) '( ))
                 (else (cons LB (nums (+ LB 1) UB)))))

7.   (define (delete_all Item L)
           (cond ((null? L) '( ))
                 ((equal? Item (car L)) (delete_all Item (cdr L)))
                 (else (cons (car L) (delete_all Item (cdr L))))))

Writing multiple functions

1.   (define (insertion_sort L)
              ; *Return a sorted version of L, using insertion sort*
              ; *Sort in descending order*
              (cond ((null? L) L)
                    ((null? (cdr L)) L)
                    (else (insert (car L) (insertion_sort (cdr L))))))

      (define (insert Item L)
              ; *Insert Item into its place in sorted list L*
              (cond ((null? L) (list Item))
                    ((>= Item (car L)) (cons Item L))
                    (else (cons (car L) (insert Item (cdr L))))))

The only difference between this function and the function for ascending insertion sort is the comparison in insert: *To sort in descending order, compare* Item *to* (car L) *using* >= *instead of* <=.

2.   (define (mode L)   ; *Return the mode of nonempty list L*
              (most_common (insertion_sort L)))

      (define (most_common L)   ; *Return the mode of sorted list L*
              (longest_sequence (cdr L) (car L) 1 (car L) 1))

      (define (longest_sequence L Curr_Item Curr_Count Mode Mode_Count)
              ; *Return mode of sorted list L, given that:*
              ; *Mode is the most common item found so far,*
              ; *Mode_Count is the number of times Mode occurs,*
              ; *Curr_Item is the item in the current sequence in the list, and*
              ; *Curr_Count is the number of times Curr_Item has been seen so far.*
              (cond ((null? L) Mode)
                    ((and (equal? (car L) Curr_Item) (>= Curr_Count Mode_Count))
                         (longest_sequence (cdr L) Curr_Item
                                 (+ 1 Curr_Count) Curr_Item (+ 1 Curr_Count)))
                    ((equal? (car L) Curr_Item)   ; *and Curr_Count < Mode_Count*
                         (longest_sequence (cdr L) Curr_Item
                                 (+ 1 Curr_Count) Mode Mode_Count))
                    (else
                         (longest_sequence (cdr L) (car L) 1 Mode Mode_Count))))

Chapter 6

Data structures

1. (define (balanced_s L S)
        (cond ((null? L) (empty? S))
                ((not (or (left_par (car L)) (right_par (car L))))
                        (balanced_s (cdr L) S))
                ((left_par (car L))
                        (balanced_s (cdr L) (push (car L) S)))
                ((and (right_par (car L)) (empty? S)) #F)
                ((and (right_par (car L)) (left_par (top S)))
                        (balanced_s (cdr L) (pop S)))
                (else #F)))

    The new code is the second predicate-expression pair in the cond, *which checks for a non-parenthesis character and calls* balanced_s *recursively with an unchanged stack if such a character is found. The remainder of the code is identical to the parenthesis-only version.*

2. (define (traverse_preorder T)
        (cond ((null? T) '( ))
                (else (cons (car T)
                            (append   (traverse_preorder (left T))
                                        (traverse_preorder (right T)))))))

3. (define (traverse_postorder T)
        (cond ((null? T) '( ))
                (else (append   (traverse_postorder (left T))
                                (append   (traverse_postorder (right T))
                                            (list (car T)))))))

4. (define (traverse_inorder T)
        (cond ((null? T) 0)
                (else (+   (traverse_inorder (left T))
                            (+   (car T)
                                (traverse_inorder (right T)))))))

Appendix 2: Scheme 48

There are a number of Scheme interpreters available, written for a variety of hardware and operating system platforms. The next few appendices describe several of these interpreters. Because I expect that most of my readers will be college students on limited budgets, I have emphasized free software in my selection; however, commercial Scheme interpreters are also available.

Scheme 48 is an interpreter written by Richard Kelsey and Jonathan Rees at NEC Research Institute, implementing the *Revised*[5] standard. The original version was written for UNIX† system environments, but a version now exists for Microsoft Windows as well.

General information about Scheme 48 can be found at http://s48.org . "A User's Guide to Scheme 48" is located at http://www.cs.hmc.edu/~fleck/envision/scheme48/user-guide.html. Information on the Windows version is given at http://www.cs.nwu.edu/groups/su/edwin/ .

To run the Scheme 48 interpreter on elvis, type **scheme48** at the UNIX shell prompt. To see a list of commands, type **,?** at the interpreter prompt. Some of the most important commands are:

,load *filename*
> Load a program from a specified file. The file name should be given without any extra punctuation (it should not be preceded by a quote or surrounded by double quotes).

,help *command*
> Get a help message about the specified command.

,trace *name*
> Begin tracing calls to function *name*. This is useful for debugging.

,untrace *name*
> Stop tracing calls to function *name*.

,exit
> Exit Scheme 48

If an exception (catastrophic error) is encountered during a program run, the program will halt, with the prompt **1>**. If you wish, debugging information about the execution can be obtained by typing **,debug**; to see available debugging commands, type **?** at the *inspect:* prompt. To return to the normal prompt and normal interpreter state, type **^D** (control-D).

Creating the program file is a separate process: Use your favorite editor (such as *emacs*, *vi*, or *pico*) to create a file containing your program, and to edit it when you find errors. One easy approach to developing Scheme programs is to open two windows on your computer — one running the interpreter, and one running the editor; go back and forth between the two windows as you alternate between editing and testing the program.

Here is a sample Scheme 48 interpreter session. It assumes that a file called *homework* has already been created that contains functions *all_even* and *even_list* as described earlier.

---

† UNIX®is a registered trademark of The Open Group.

In the script below, the UNIX shell prompt is a number followed by a %, and the Scheme48 prompt is a > symbol. The computer's output is shown in Courier type, and the user's input is shown in **bold Courier** type.

The session is begun by typing scheme48 at the UNIX shell prompt. The program file is loaded, using the ,load command; then each function is tested on some sample data. To illustrate debugging, the ,trace command is used on function even_list. At the end, the session is ended with the ,exit command.

```
1% scheme48
Welcome to Scheme 48 0.46 (made by root on Sat Feb 13 04:40:34 GMT 1999).
Copyright (c) 1993, 1994 by Richard Kelsey and Jonathan Rees.
Copyright (c) 1996 by NEC Research Institute, Inc.
Please report bugs to scheme-48-bugs@martigny.ai.mit.edu.
Type ,? (comma question-mark) for help.
> ,load homework
homework
> (all_even '(3 9 10 2))
#f
> (even_list '(3 9 10 2))
 '(10 2)
> ,trace even_list
> (even_list '(3 9 10 2))
[Enter (even_list '(3 9 10 2))
[Enter (even_list '(9 10 2))
[Enter (even_list '(10 2))
[Enter (even_list '(2))
[Enter (even_list '())
 Leave even_list '()]
 Leave even_list '(2)]
 Leave even_list '(10 2)]
 Leave even_list '(10 2)]
 Leave even_list '(10 2)]
 '(10 2)
> ,exit
2%
```

Appendix 3: DrScheme

DrScheme is an interpreter written at Rice University for students learning Scheme. It provides several versions of Scheme, tailored to different levels of expertise: *Beginning Student, Intermediate Student, Advanced Student,* and *Full Scheme.* The student versions of the language apply extra restrictions and error-checking features to help diagnose and correct some of the errors that beginners are likely to make. *Full Scheme* provides an implementation of the *Revised⁵ Report* Scheme standard, plus some additional features not in the standard, including exceptions and tools for GUI applications. Implementations of DrScheme are available for several UNIX systems, several versions of Windows, and the Macintosh. The software is covered under the GNU Lesser General Public License.

The DrScheme home page at http://www.cs.rice.edu/CS/PLT/packages/drscheme/ gives information about the history of DrScheme, instructions for using DrScheme, and locations for downloading the software. It also includes links to two papers published about DrScheme: "DrScheme: a pedagogic programming environment for Scheme", by Robert Bruce Findler, Cormac Flanagan, Matthew Flatt, Shriram Krishnamurthi, and Matthias Felleisen (*Proceedings of the 1997 Symposium on Programming Languages: Implementations, Logics, and Programs*) and "The DrScheme Project: An Overview, by Matthias Felleisen, Robert Bruce Findler, Matthew Flatt, and Shriram Krishnamurthi" (*SIGPLAN Notices*, June 1998).

DrScheme gives the user an integrated development environment. A code window and an execution window are displayed side-by-side, and when a run-time error occurs in execution, the offending portion of the program is highlighted in the code window. Loading, saving, language-level selection, and most other commands occur through menu choices. DrScheme includes an extensive tutorial on the DrScheme software, available by selecting *Help/Welcome to DrScheme/Take a Tour!* from the menu.

Below is an image of a DrScheme session. Functions `all_even` and `even_list` have been loaded, and the functions are executed on some test data. Note the response when `even_list` is called with a parameter of 12, instead of a list, resulting in the attempt to compute the `car` of a number: a bug symbol is displayed, with a message explaining the type mismatch. The word *car* in the error message is a hyperlink to a definition of the `car` function.

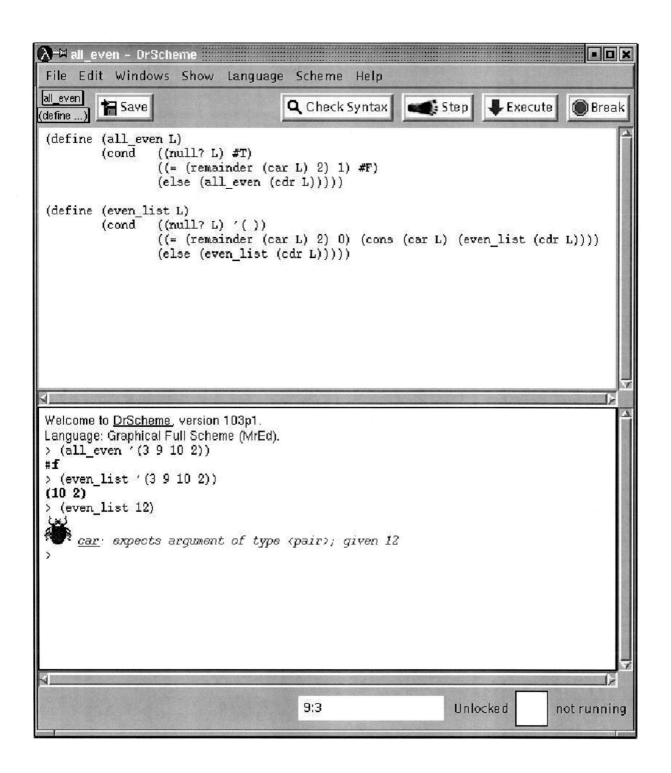

```
(define (all_even L)
        (cond   ((null? L) #T)
                ((= (remainder (car L) 2) 1) #F)
                (else (all_even (cdr L)))))

(define (even_list L)
        (cond   ((null? L) '( ))
                ((= (remainder (car L) 2) 0) (cons (car L) (even_list (cdr L))))
                (else (even_list (cdr L)))))
```

Welcome to DrScheme, version 103p1.
Language: Graphical Full Scheme (MrEd).
> (all_even '(3 9 10 2))
#f
> (even_list '(3 9 10 2))
(10 2)
> (even_list 12)

    car: *expects argument of type ⟨pair⟩; given 12*
>

Appendix 4: Chez Scheme

Chez Scheme is a commercial Scheme compiler developed by Cadence Research Systems. It implements the standard in the *Revised⁵ Report*, along with a number of additional features. Petite Chez Scheme is a free Scheme interpreter, also from Cadence Research Systems; it is compatible with Chez Scheme but uses an interpreter rather than a compiler.

The web site for Chez Scheme, http://www.scheme.com/ , provides links for downloading Petite Chez Scheme, contact information for licensing Chez Scheme, an electronic version of the *Chez Scheme User's Guide*, by R. Kent Dybvig, and an electronic version of *The Scheme Programming Language*, also by R. Kent Dybvig.

Petite Chez Scheme in a UNIX environment, like many other interpreters and compilers for UNIX systems, does not include an editor; instead, the programmer creates the program separately, using his or her favorite editor (such as *emacs*, *vi*, or *pico*), then loads the program file into the interpreter.

Some of the important Petite Chez Scheme commands are:

(load *filename***)**
> Load a program from a specified file. The file name should be surrounded by double quotes.

(trace *name***)**
> Begin tracing calls to function *name*. This is useful for debugging.

(untrace *fname***)**
> Stop tracing calls to function *name*.

(exit)
> Exit the interpreter

Here is a sample Petite Chez Scheme interpreter session. It assumes that a file called *homework* has already been created that contains functions *all_even* and *even_list* as described earlier.

In the script below, the UNIX shell prompt is a number followed by a %, and the Petite Chez Scheme prompt is a > symbol. The computer's output is shown in Courier type, and the user's input is shown in **bold Courier** type.

The session is begun by typing petite at the UNIX shell prompt. The program file is loaded, using the load command; then each function is tested on some sample data. To illustrate debugging, the trace command is used on function even_list. At the end, the session is ended with the exit command.

```
1% petite
Petite Chez Scheme Version 6.0a
Copyright (c) 1998 Cadence Research Systems

> (load "homework")
> (all_even '(3 9 10 2))
#f
> (even_list '(3 9 10 2))
(10 2)
> (trace even_list)
(even_list)
> (even_list '(3 9 10 2))
|(even_list (3 9 10 2))
|(even_list (9 10 2))
|(even_list (10 2))
| (even_list (2))
| |(even_list ())
| |()
| (2)
|(10 2)
(10 2)
> (exit)
2%
```

Appendix 5: MIT Scheme

MIT Scheme is an interpreter developed at MIT, with versions available for UNIX, OS/2, and Windows. It is free software, available under the GNU General Public License. The MIT Scheme home page at http://www.swiss.ai.mit.edu/projects/scheme/mit/ contains information about the interpreter and links for downloading the software. The MIT Scheme User's Manual is located at http://www.swiss.ai.mit.edu/projects/scheme/documentation/user.html , and the Reference Manual is at http://www.swiss.ai.mit.edu/projects/scheme/documentation/scheme.html .

Interpreter commands include:

(load *filename*)

> Load a program from a specified file. The file name should be surrounded by double quotes.

(trace *name*)

> Begin tracing calls to function *name*. This is useful for debugging.

(trace-entry *name*), **(trace_exit** *name*)

> Trace the entry and exit points (respectively) of function *name*.

(untrace *fname*)

> Stop tracing calls to function *name*.

(trace-entry *name*), **(trace_exit** *name*)

> Stop tracing the entry and exit points (respectively) of function *name*.

(break-entry *name*)

> Set a break point at the entry to function *name*.

(break-exit *name*)

> Set a break point at the exit from function *name*.

(unbreak-entry *name*)

> Clear the break point at the entry to function *name*.

(unbreak-exit *name*)

> Clear the break point at the exit from function *name*.

(unbreak *name*)

> Clear all break points for function *name*.

(exit)

> Exit the interpreter

(quit)

> Suspend the interpreter (similar to ˆZ on UNIX systems)

The MIT Scheme interpreter is a separate tool which does not include an editor. To use MIT Scheme, first create the program file using your favorite editor (*emacs*, *vi*, etc.). After saving the program, run the interpreter and load the program using the *load* command.

Below is a sample MIT Scheme interpreter session. It assumes that a file called *homework* has already been created that contains functions *all_even* and *even_list* as described earlier.

In the script below, the UNIX shell prompt is a number followed by a %, and the MIT Scheme prompt is a > symbol. The computer's output is shown in Courier type, and the user's input is shown in **bold Courier** type.

The session is begun by typing scheme at the UNIX shell prompt. The program file is loaded, using the load command; then each function is tested on some sample data. To illustrate debugging, the trace command is used on function even_list. At the end, the session is ended with the exit command. (And, yes, MIT Scheme really does print Happy Happy Joy Joy when it exits.)

```
1% scheme
Scheme Microcode Version 14.5
MIT Scheme running under FreeBSD
Type '^C' (control-C) followed by 'H' to obtain information about
interrupts.
Scheme saved on Tuesday November 27, 2001 at 1:53:32 AM
   Release 7.6.0
   Microcode 14.5
   Runtime 14.192

1 ]=> (load "homework")

;Loading "homework" -- done
;Value: even_list

1 ]=> (all_even '(3 9 10 2))

;Value: ()

1 ]=> (all_even '(2 4 6 8))

;Value: #t

1 ]=> (even_list '(3 9 10 2))

;Value 1: (10 2)

1 ]=> (trace even_list)

;Unspecified return value

1 ]=> (even_list '(3 9 10 2))

[Entering #[compound-procedure 2 even_list]
    Args: (3 9 10 2)]
[Entering #[compound-procedure 2 even_list]
    Args: (9 10 2)]
[Entering #[compound-procedure 2 even_list]
```

```
    Args: (10 2)]
[Entering #[compound-procedure 2 even_list]
    Args: (2)]
[Entering #[compound-procedure 2 even_list]
    Args: ()]
[()
        <== #[compound-procedure 2 even_list]
    Args: ()]
[(2)
        <== #[compound-procedure 2 even_list]
    Args: (2)]
[(10 2)
        <== #[compound-procedure 2 even_list]
    Args: (10 2)]
[(10 2)
        <== #[compound-procedure 2 even_list]
    Args: (9 10 2)]
[(10 2)
        <== #[compound-procedure 2 even_list]
    Args: (3 9 10 2)]
;Value 3: (10 2)

1 ]=> (exit)

Kill Scheme (y or n)? Yes
Happy Happy Joy Joy.

2%
```

Index